HIRING

MADE EASY AS PIE

Praise for **Hiring Made Easy as PIE**

"I have been involved in helping organizations hire right for over 30 years and can honestly say Dr. Johnson's book is the most practical and easy to use resource I've found. He writes in an easy-to-read combination of stories and step-by-step checklists that cut to the chase. If you want to increase your probability of hiring the best-fit employee the first time, read this book. This is the book on the topic. I highly recommend it."

— Henry L. Thompson, Ph.D.,
President & CEO, High Performing Systems, Inc.

"Hiring highly qualified people who are also the right fit for your organization's culture is one of leadership's greatest challenges. Alonzo's book provides a thorough and effective process to ensure your success. His experience, insights and examples will guide you every step of the way!"

— Jeff Peden, M.Ed., leadership consultant and
author of *How to Grow Your Business Without Spending Money*

"If you think hiring the right person is hard work, then Alonzo Johnson's *Hiring Made Easy as PIE* should be at the top of your reading list. Whether you hire one person a year or an entire team of employees each month, Johnson's book gives practical, step-by-step instructions on how to select the person who will best fit with your organization. It's a fun and easy read . . . as easy as PIE!"

— Cathy Fyock, CSP, SPHR, author of
The Truth About Hiring the Best, Hiring Source Book, and *Get the Best*

"Alonzo Johnson's book is the go-to guide for hiring! It is perfect for any manager, new or seasoned, needing to hire the best candidate for his or her organization. Alonzo uses a step-by-step approach and provides real-world examples throughout the book that address the many uncertainties that can come with making a hiring decision. *Hiring Made Easy as PIE* offers a quick reference guide and other tools to help hiring managers select the best-fit person for the job, while making the hiring process easier."

— William S. Dang, Learning Technology Director, LOMA

"A recipe for success—Alonzo Johnson's *Hiring Made Easy as PIE* is a must-have for the manager engaged in any phase of the hiring process. This book takes the critical task of hiring your most important resource and breaks it down into an understandable and workable plan. Alonzo's insights and real-world scenarios provide answers and direction for all of us involved in strengthening our organizations with great employees."

— Michael Goldberg,
Former Senior VP of Human Resources, Fortune 500 Organization

"'Oh no! Another how-to book to read. I'm already very busy and I'm also tasked with finding and hiring a new employee.' If that's your first thought, think again because this book is a well-crafted and easy read that will assure that you get the right person for the job, the right way. Based on Alonzo's success with recruiting, hiring, and retaining top employees for major organizations, *Hiring Made Easy as PIE* has everything you'll need to know to get the job done."

— Boyd Watkins, President, Interel, Inc.

"This is an invaluable book for both HR and non-HR managers who are expected to interview and hire best-fit candidates to fill job openings. It is also a must-read for managers who have to recruit individuals within the larger organization to build a project team. Although the book touches on all the complexities of the hiring process, it is written in a way that makes it fun to read and easy to follow. I especially liked the fact that very practical and succinct examples are provided for the topics and situations discussed. I will definitely use this book as a guide every time I am involved in the hiring process."

— Alberta A. Boakye, PMP, Senior Project Manager, Genesys

"*Hiring Made Easy as PIE* provides a clear and concise road map for candidate selection. The PIE methodology can help transform a frequently chaotic experience, full of chance and gut feeling, into a practical repeatable process. I found myself nodding in agreement as Alonzo presented perspectives I may not have given appropriate attention to in the past. This is a great tune-up for seasoned hiring managers and a terrific guide for newcomers—I recommend it for job-seekers as well!"

— David Coonfare, Senior IT Professional

"Finally, a how-to book on hiring that is not only informative but enjoyable to read. Alonzo presents stories about his personal hiring experiences and other vignettes that bring this book to life. As one with a responsibility for hiring, I find this book invaluable. It presents such a refreshingly simple yet effective approach to hiring that is indeed easy as PIE."

— Carl Paschall, Assistant Manager, Sherwin-Williams Paints

"*Hiring Made Easy as PIE* is a great book for a small business owner like me. I am going through rounds of hiring right now and don't have an HR manager. This book answered questions I had and taught me things that I hadn't even thought about before entering the interviewing and hiring process. I highly recommended it for leaders who have to do most of their own hiring."

— Joe DeSensi, Ed.D., President and Co-Founder of Informatics Direct and Professor of Leadership Studies, Webster University and Spalding University

"You'll quickly learn in this book why your 'gut feeling' is not nearly enough on which to base your next hiring decision. Taking the time up front to critically evaluate and validate how the new hire can really add value to your organization is so often missed across hiring managers and HR professionals alike! *Hiring Made Easy as PIE* should be required reading for anyone with the responsibility for hiring."

— AJ Holley, Director of Change Management & Learning, Changepoint

HIRING

MADE EASY AS PIE

The Hiring Manager's Guide to Selecting the Best-Fit Employee

Alonzo Johnson, Ph.D.

OASYS Press ◊ McDonough, GA

Hiring Made Easy as PIE:
The Hiring Manager's Guide to Selecting the Best-Fit Employee

Printed in the United States of America
First Edition, 2015

21 20 19 18 17 16 15 1 2 3 4 5

978-0-9863965-0-2 (paperback)
978-0-9863965-1-9 (e-book)

Visit the author's websites:
www.HiringMadeEasyasPIE.com
www.TheOASYSGroup.com

Cover design by Kevin Williamson and Tudor Maier
Book layout by Kevin Williamson

◊ ◊ ◊ ◊ ◊

Hiring Made Easy as PIE is available for sale at special quantity discounts. For more information, please visit HiringMadeEasyasPIE.com, or send inquiries to Alonzo@TheOASYSGroup.com.

Contents

Preface

Hiring best-fit employees has always been critical to organizational success. Changes in today's workforce have caused employers to focus more sharply on this critical task.

Of course, there is no shortage of literature on the realities of the changing workforce landscape, but let's review it anyway. As of January 2011, Baby Boomers (people born between 1946 and 1964) began turning 65 years old. Approximately 10,000 seasoned employees are exiting the workplace every day, as more Baby Boomers reach retirement age. And, according to the Pew Research Center, this trend is expected to continue until the year 2030. The result will be a deficit in skill and experience that will challenge employers for decades.

Organizational leaders are keenly aware that effective hiring practices directly relate to the achievement of their goals. Without a structured process for hiring best-fit employees who can replace these retiring Baby Boomers, leaders run the risk of bankrupting their organizations of human capital.

So what is being done to shore up this very important part of the business given the impending shortage of qualified employees?

In the not-so-distant past, Human Resources (HR) was responsible for making most hiring decisions. In the interest of empowering leaders and streamlining HR functions, many organizations are trending towards delegating the lion's share of hiring responsibilities to line managers and supervisors. Today, line managers and supervisors are often front-and-center of the hiring process—even more so than the official

HR function—from writing job advertisements and interviewing, to making the final hiring decision. With all of these responsibilities shifted to the line manager or supervisor, how do companies ensure that these managers use an effective, yet lawful approach to select best-fit employees?

Hiring is important, but it doesn't need to be daunting or complex. In this book, I've applied my experience and research on hiring to present a methodical approach for hiring that is easily learned and applied. After many years in the hiring and talent management business world, I have synthesized my knowledge of hiring into these essential teachings for those with the responsibility of making important hiring decisions. With this book as your guide, hiring truly can be as easy (and enjoyable) as PIE.

Acknowledgements

Numerous people have contributed to this book. Without their help, it would not have been possible.

I am especially grateful to Annmarie Buchanan. Her encouragement of me to start this project and guidance throughout the writing process was invaluable.

I would like to acknowledge a few very accomplished human resources professionals: Susan Putlock, Marigrace McKay, and Michael Goldberg, for providing vital feedback on the content of this book. I am also most appreciative to Michael Goldberg for sharing his knowledge of hiring with me over the years as my boss and as my mentor. Thank you for believing in me and for allowing me to lead a corporate staffing function under your tutelage!

A big 'thank you' to Nancy Nimz, employment law attorney, for reviewing and validating the legal elements contained throughout this book.

To Jeff Corkran, Joe DeSensi, Whitney Martin, and Kevin Williamson for their help with editing this book; for others who took time to review and provide valuable feedback—thank you!

I would also like to recognize the many participants who attended my workshops on hiring over the years—thank you for challenging and inspiring me to grow.

I am sincerely grateful!

Introduction

Empathize for a moment with Jon Alson, a manager who has just received a major assignment which he must finish within the next two months. Jon's unit is already short-staffed from the recent department restructuring, and each team member has been asked to perform duties that were split between two or more employees. There is more work than the team can handle and Jon is in desperate need of help. Jon's boss just gave him the go-ahead to hire someone for a newly approved position that will report directly to him.

While delighted that help is on the horizon, Jon realizes that he has never hired anyone before. He promptly makes his way to the HR office to seek assistance with filling the position. Jon assumes that if he just lets the HR office know what he needs, the staff in the office would take it from there. Reality, however, shapes up to be quite different from what Jon had assumed.

Jon explains the job requirements to the HR manager, who asks him to write an advertisement for the position to be posted in the local media. Jon does so. Within a week of posting the advertisement, résumés start rolling in. Shortly thereafter, Jon is summoned to HR and is presented with a stack of résumés. He is asked to screen the résumés and then select candidates to be interviewed.

Jon does his best to screen the résumés and selects those he thinks showed promise for the new position. He uses the résumés to conduct phone screenings to create a short list of candidates to interview. Jon interviews candidates from his short list and is able to select the one he believes is the best-qualified. Jon extends the offer.

Having not hired anyone before, Jon feels he did the best that he could, given the scant support and guidance he received from HR. The employee accepts the job . . . but resigns a few months later as other opportunities come his way.

A Twist of Familiarity

Is this scenario familiar to you? Well, it is to me. Jon was me (or I was Jon) early in my business career. That experience was my introduction to the world of hiring. Like many leaders with the responsibility of hiring, I had not been trained to interview and select employees. I was uneasy about the hiring process in general and about what I should or should not ask during the interview, especially from a legal standpoint.

Since that time, I have developed an insatiable curiosity for learning how to hire most effectively, and I have continued to hone my hiring prowess over the years. I have led staffing efforts for Fortune 500 companies and have continued to research ways to simplify and improve the hiring process. My doctoral dissertation was dedicated to researching the influence of personality and ideal candidate work behaviors on applicant attraction to jobs.

My days as an unskilled hiring manager are over, but as I continue to conduct workshops on effective hiring practices, I often meet leaders who, like me early in my business career, want to improve their skills in identifying and selecting best-fit employees.

WHO SHOULD READ THIS BOOK

This book is intended for anyone who needs to hire someone to fill a position in the workplace. It is written for any non-HR person with a hiring responsibility, who does not have dedicated HR support. Accordingly, this book will provide readers with an easy-to-understand approach that is designed to help those with limited hiring skills to fulfill their critical hiring role.

HOW TO USE THIS BOOK

Hiring Made Easy as PIE is a how-to guide for hiring. It presents PIE as an acronym for hiring in three slices or three phases—Prepare, Interview, and Evaluate.

There are three options for navigating this book:
1. Read it from cover to cover;
2. Read only the slice you need to enhance your knowledge;
3. Review any part of it as a reference.

This book also offers sample questions and forms as aids that may be used during interviews, as well as other tools that can be used throughout the hiring process.

A Structured Hiring Process as Easy as PIE

So you have gotten the green light to add someone to your team. This feeling is usually met with mixed emotions. You are relieved and grateful that management notices just how much work you have to do with so few resources. Because you've needed this person since at least a couple months ago, it's very important that you get someone who can hit the ground running.

If this person does not deliver, you might end up with even more work than when you started, and your team's morale will suffer even more. So what do you do?

First
As you prepare for your hiring journey, make sure that you follow a structured process that will yield answers to the following three questions:

A. **Can the candidate do the job (the "Can")?** Does the candidate have the required skills, knowledge, education, and experience for this position? Is he or she able to articulate real experiences and information to demonstrate that he or she can do the job?

B. **Will the candidate do the job (the "Will")?** Is the candidate motivated? Are job requirements consistent with what the candidate enjoys doing? Do the career objectives of this person align with the duties of the job, or are there advancement opportunities for him or her? Does the candidate's job history show the type of upward advancement you would expect of him or her?

C. **Is the candidate a good fit for the culture within the organization (the "Fit")?** Does the candidate's work behavior, style and personality mesh with the job and the company?

Second

I emphasized earlier that the process should be a structured one. A structured process is designed to unearth job-related information and should directly link the interview questions to the job requirements. An ad hoc, willy-nilly approach to hiring can put your company at risk for certain kinds of legal action—and will likely not produce the best-fit employee.

Did you know that a candidate selection tool (like the interview and evaluation forms that you use) is considered a competency test and is governed by guidelines found in the Principles for the Validation and Use of Personnel Selection Procedures, Fourth Edition? These guidelines are developed by the Society for Industrial and Organizational Psychology (SIOP) and can be found online. While these guidelines have not been mandated by law, they have been referenced in several court cases and are viewed by the courts as a source of technical information and authority on employment matters. Your selection instruments are held to the same standards as a competency test and must have reliability and validity.

✓ **Validity (accuracy)** is the degree to which an instrument measures what it is supposed to measure. In the case of the interview: does it predict job performance by measuring a candidate's skills, knowledge, experience, and work behavior for a specific job?

✓ **Reliability (consistency)** is the extent to which an instrument yields consistent results. For an interview, that would mean: does the instrument yield consistent information that can be used to select the best-fit candidate, even if different people are conducting interviews?

So what is that structured process that will answer the three questions we just discussed, and that will meet those guidelines?

Could it be that this structured process is as easy as PIE? I think so!

Again, PIE stands for **PREPARE, INTERVIEW** and **EVALUATE**. For the remainder of this book, we will examine the tasks or activities that constitute this very simple but structured process.

Let's start with the **PREPARE** phase!

The First Slice—PREPARE

"Time spent on hiring is time well spent."
— Robert Half

Preparing to hire is undoubtedly the most time-consuming part of the hiring process, but well worth it in the end. Think about your favorite dessert that you like to make—a pie, for example. It did not become a pie by accident. Every pie takes planning and preparation before you can actually enjoy it.

Did you know that the term "easy as pie" does not mean as easy as making pie? It really means as easy as eating pie. The hiring process presented in this book is simple and yields results, but you still have to do the work. Taking the time to prepare will yield better results for you, if you seek to hire a best-fit employee and benefit your organization in the long run.

Why is proper preparation so important? How does it help to hire the best-fit employee?

Proper preparation streamlines the search for the best-fit employee, it reduces the chances for adverse legal actions, and it provides a roadmap that makes follow-through and collaboration within the hiring process more manageable.

So what steps are involved in preparing to hire your next best-fit employee?

The steps are:

- ☐ **Identify Job Scope and Requirements**
- ☐ **Review Other Job Specifications**
- ☐ **Determine Culture Fit Requirements**
- ☐ **Write the Job Advertisement**
- ☐ **Develop Applicant Pool**
- ☐ **Screen Résumés**
- ☐ **Develop Interview Questions**
- ☐ **Plan the Interview**

During this phase, you may interface with the HR office if you have one, but most of the tasks in this phase will be carried out by you, the hiring manager.

Let's start our discussion with identifying the scope of the job and identifying what you'll require from prospective job applicants.

IDENTIFY JOB SCOPE AND REQUIREMENTS

Identifying the job's scope and requirements is the first step in the PREPARE phase of the process. To accomplish it, you must first conduct a thorough review of the current job description. This review helps to pinpoint job-related information that you will use later to (A) advertise the job, (B) screen résumés, and (C) interview candidates.

Before you get started, verify that the job description is up to date; positions do change over time, so the scope and requirements may have changed. If you are not thoroughly familiar with the job, talk to someone who may know more about the job scope and requirements. Consider talking to someone who is currently in the role, like a subject matter expert (SME), or a downstream internal customer.

If this is a new position, you will need to develop a job description. Your HR office might be able to provide you with a template to get you started, or you can go to The **O**ccupational Information **Net**work (www.onet.com). ONET is a free online service that you can use to find job descriptions that you can modify to meet your needs.

Always view the hiring process as an opportunity to find the best-fit employee who can grow with the organization. When preparing to hire, it is imperative to take a forward-looking approach when determining your needs for the position. Otherwise, you risk hiring someone only for today's needs, someone without the capacity to grow further in the role as its demands grow with the company.

Remember, you need to make this hire count! Think about all the ways this person could add value and improve your team's performance. You will need to think about the core knowledge and skills that you need (and would prefer) him or her to have.

First, look at your own objectives for the next 12 months and longer-term, if you have them available. Next, ask yourself: what duties will I assign this new employee? Then, based on all the tasks that I need accomplished, what will be required of the new employee to fulfill the scope of work, complement the team and successfully accomplish assigned team objectives?

The following is a list of considerations for identifying job scope and requirements. Let's discuss each.

Knowledge and Skills Requirements (the "Can")

Remember that knowledge and skills are not interchangeable; experience differentiates the two. For example, an administrative assistant can have "knowledge of" word processing and database management software, but it does not mean that he or she is effective at producing easy-to-read correspondences or building a database. It simply means that he or she knows the software. However, an experienced administrative assistant with knowledge of the software applications is likely to have the skills to be more effective at producing easy-to-read correspondences and building a database.

To further clarify my point, the following are actual examples, taken from ONET, of some of the top knowledge and skills requirements for an Administrative Assistant. (We'll be using this position as an extended example for discussing your hiring needs.)

Knowledge
- ✓ Clerical—knowledge of word processing, managing records, transcribing, and designing forms.
- ✓ English Language—knowledge of English language including the meaning and spelling of words, rules of composition and style, and professional grammar.
- ✓ Customer and Personal Service—knowledge of principles and processes for providing customer and personal services.

Skills
- ✓ Writing—communicating effectively in writing to various audiences.
- ✓ Active Listening—giving full attention to what other people are saying, taking time to understand, appropriately asking and responding to questions.
- ✓ Reading Comprehension—fully comprehending written documents.
- ✓ Speaking—effectively conveying information through speech.
- ✓ Time Management—managing one's own time and the time of others.

As you can see from the above examples, knowledge and skills are not synonymous. When reviewing the job description to identify knowledge and skills requirements, make sure you examine the two terms independently.

Duties and Responsibilities

Now that you have determined what knowledge and skills the ideal candidate should possess, decide what he or she will actually do; these are otherwise known as duties and responsibilities. This decision will determine what role the employee will play in the organization. Following our previous example, the duties and responsibilities of an Administrative Assistant as identified by ONET include the following:

- ✓ Use computers for various applications, such as database management or word processing.
- ✓ Answer telephones and give information to callers, take messages, or transfer calls to appropriate individuals.
- ✓ Create, maintain, and enter information into databases.
- ✓ Set up and manage paper or electronic filing systems, recording information, updating paperwork, or maintaining documents, such as attendance records, correspondence, or other material.
- ✓ Operate office equipment, such as fax machines, copiers, or phone systems and arrange for repairs when equipment malfunctions.
- ✓ Greet visitors or callers and handle their inquiries or direct them to the appropriate persons according to their needs.
- ✓ Maintain scheduling and event calendars.
- ✓ Complete forms in accordance with company procedures.
- ✓ Schedule and confirm appointments for clients, customers, or supervisors.
- ✓ Make copies of correspondence or other printed material.

It is essential for you, as the hiring manager, to know the required duties and responsibilities of a job because they provide insight into the employee's role in the organization, and will allow you to develop relevant interview questions that ultimately lead to hiring the best-fit candidate for the job.

Educational and Experience Prerequisites

Based on what you have decided are the important knowledge, skills, and duties for the position, which do you think is more important: education or work experience? Which makes a better employee?

Although this debate has circulated throughout the business world for a long time, there is not one conclusive answer. During my tenure as a staffing and development executive, even I could not conclusively answer this question. Almost every time I hired for a position reporting directly to me, my boss and I debated the importance of education versus experience for the job. When two candidates were equally qualified in all other areas, I usually selected the person with the most education rather than the person with the most experience.

My rationale was that my department developed and administered a number of specialized tools internally, including employee 360-degree assessments and employee engagement surveys. In the process, we used statistics to validate and analyze data. I needed people who understood statistics as well as I did or better.

But this is only one example of how you can weigh education and work experience when filling specific roles. Both are important; whether one seems more important than the other depends on the job. As the hiring manager, you should always weigh these factors carefully against the requirements of the job.

Relevant Work Behaviors (the "Fit")

Often referred to as the "it factor" by some, work behaviors are characteristics individuals possess that are necessary for their success in organizations. Have you ever met an employee who possessed all the requisite skills, knowledge, and education, but who still was not considered a great employee?

It boils down to this: the "how" is just as important (if not more important) as the "what" in performing a job. Work behaviors can include characteristics such as assertiveness, independence, stress tolerance, interpersonal skills, or a specific personality trait. These intangible requirements can sometimes be difficult to identify when you are meeting someone for the first time, especially in an interview setting when the candidate is usually seeking to make a positive impression on the interviewer.

When preparing to hire someone, be careful not to overlook work behavior requirements. Though otherwise qualified, a candidate who is lacking in these important requirements is not a good fit for the organization. Compared to a candidate with the required work behaviors, he or she is more likely to derail if hired. Let's talk a little about what it means to derail.

Derailment occurs when an employee's career stalls because he or she has failed to perform as expected. Derailment often results in the employee exiting the organization, often involuntarily. I learned about derailment first-hand, while working in corporate America. As the lead talent management executive, my boss asked me to determine why some employees derailed and left the company.

After reviewing the records of terminated employees, I was surprised to find that none of them derailed due to a lack of technical skills and competency (the knowledge and skills we just discussed); they all derailed due to a lack of one or more work behaviors. In this case, I found the lack of interpersonal skills and inability to work independently to be the primary reasons why employees derailed and left the company.

As the hiring manager, make sure you review the job at the beginning of the hiring process to determine how it will be required to function within your culture. Then, identify what "it factors," or work behaviors, are necessary for an employee to be successful in that role within your organization.

The "gray area" work behavior question...

So are you still wondering about what the "it" factor is for the position you are trying to fill?

Maybe this example will help. When I was leading a global staffing and development function in the corporate world, my department often had to deal with ambiguous situations or "gray areas." Employees of the department needed to be able to handle them. So every candidate whom I interviewed to work with us was asked a question that would assess his or her ability to deal with gray areas.

An example of a fit requirement question that I asked was: "Tell me about a time when you had to make a decision and/or operate in a gray area. How did you go about doing it? What was the outcome?"

I have never hired a candidate who could not answer such a question well. Because we sometimes had to operate between the lines of policy or procedure for a given task—within the gray area—I needed team members who could function there. I knew this was important because of my experiences with employees who did not deal well with ambiguity; such employees had difficulty filling in the blanks and making gray-area decisions.

Reporting Relationships

Many of today's organizations have complex reporting relationships. Larger organizations usually have more complex reporting relationships than smaller ones.

Many organizations use a matrix structure. In a matrix structure, one employee may report to multiple bosses. For example, an Administrative Assistant who reports directly to the VP of Marketing might also report indirectly to the Director of Customer Service. For the sake of this example, let's say that the Administrative Assistant provides 60% support to the VP of Marketing and 40% support to the Director of Customer Service. This direct and indirect reporting relationship reflects the proportion of time provided to each leader and allows both of them to manage a portion of the Administrative Assistant's time and provide weighted performance review input accordingly.

Understanding the reporting relationships is important if you want to find an employee who is the right fit for the job and culture. When filling a vacant position, the hiring manager should answer the following questions early in the hiring process:

A. Who will this employee report to directly?
B. Will this employee report to anyone indirectly?
C. Will this employee have direct and or indirect reports?
D. Will the boss of this employee have other direct or indirect employees reporting to him or her?
E. Will this employee have to influence others to get work done without authority?

Answers to these questions will begin to paint a picture of the ideal work behaviors for the best-fit person for the job and the culture.

How the job relates to the work environment—what, how, and with whom the employee will interact within the organization—is another key consideration for finding the employee who is the right fit. Answering the vital questions below will aid the hiring manager in identifying how the job will relate to the work environment:

A. How will this new employee relate to other employees in the organization?
B. Who is responsible for providing this employee with key resources such as information and data? Upon whom will this employee rely?
C. At what "level of authority" within the organization will this employee communicate?
D. What kind of support, if any, will this employee provide across the organization?

Hiring managers should also consider the physical and mental requirements of the job, including safety. Finding the employee who will relate well to the work environment (both job and culture) creates an engaging environment. This makes for a happier employee and a more productive workplace all around.

Any Special Job Requirements

Some jobs have special requirements such as language, interpersonal skills, strong written and verbal communication skills, and even the ability to lift a specific amount of weight. Clearly identify in the job description any special requirements that are necessary to perform the job. If you believe there are special requirements that are not spelled out in the job description, you should discuss this with HR or whoever is responsible for keeping job descriptions accurate and up to date. Make sure these requirements are added to the written job description. If there is no job description for the job and you are not certain about the special requirements, you should ask a subject matter expert (SME) about any special requirements. Any such requirements must be consistently applied to all applicants.

By the way, you should have written down all of the information you have identified thus far about job scope and requirements. To capture this information, many organizations create customized forms. Once filled in, these forms help you, the hiring manager, to focus clearly on the job requirements throughout the hiring process. Standardized forms not only provide structure, they add important validity and reliability. Remember our discussion about validity and reliability? The Hiring Workbook, shown on page 20, is an example of standardized forms that I have used to capture job scope and requirements information. (It's available on the book's website as well.) At this point, you should have enough information to begin populating the Skills & Knowledge and Work Behavior sections of the workbook.

You can use the Hiring Workbook throughout the hiring process. Not only is it used to capture job skills, requirements, and scope during the initial job analysis, it is also used to evaluate the candidate's qualifications in conjunction with his or her résumé before the interview. Additionally, it is used to evaluate the candidate's performance during and after the interview. The use of this workbook, along with well-developed interview questions, will help you identify the best-fit candidate for the job and organization.

Skills & Knowledge and Work Behavior Sections of Hiring Workbook
(Partially Completed)

Candidate Name _____ **Position** Administrative Asst.

> **INSTRUCTIONS**: Review the job description to identify the Skills & Knowledge and Work Behaviors required to successfully perform in this position. Write the Skills & Knowledge (the "Can") and Work Behaviors (the "Fit") in the spaces provided. Rate the candidate on each of these components (by placing a check in the appropriate box) during the interview or immediately following the interview. Use the comments area to write notes about the candidate. Note the candidate's motivation ("the Will") to do the job in the space provided on page 3 along with his or her strengths, weaknesses, overall rating, and the hiring decision.

Required Skills & Knowledge (THE "CAN")	VERY STRONG	STRONG	AVERAGE	WEAK	VERY WEAK	COMMENTS
Communications (Written & Verbal)	☐	☐	☐	☐	☐	
Clerical Competency	☐	☐	☐	☐	☐	
Organization/Planning/Prioritization	☐	☐	☐	☐	☐	
Critical Thinking	☐	☐	☐	☐	☐	
Attention to Detail	☐	☐	☐	☐	☐	
Database Development & Mgmt.	☐	☐	☐	☐	☐	
SharePoint Development & Mgmt.	☐	☐	☐	☐	☐	
Office Management	☐	☐	☐	☐	☐	

Required Work Behaviors (THE "FIT")	VERY STRONG	STRONG	AVERAGE	WEAK	VERY WEAK
Approachability	☐	☐	☐	☐	☐
Interpersonal Relationships	☐	☐	☐	☐	☐
Self-Awareness	☐	☐	☐	☐	☐
Learning Agility and Innovation	☐	☐	☐	☐	☐
Dealing With Ambiguity	☐	☐	☐	☐	☐
Managing Diversity	☐	☐	☐	☐	☐
Flexibility	☐	☐	☐	☐	☐
Stress Tolerance	☐	☐	☐	☐	☐

REVIEW OTHER JOB SPECIFICATIONS

You should also review other job specifications during this step. Knowing these specifications allows you to be prepared for questions from the candidate during the interview. In many organizations, this information is captured on a Personnel Action Form (PAF) or Request to Fill (RTF) form that HR helps the hiring manager complete (that is, when you request a new position or request to fill a vacancy). Ask someone from the HR department for the PAF for the position (if you have an HR department).

The checklist below consists of additional job specifications that you should become familiar with during the preparation phase.

✓ Exemption Status of the Job

Under the Federal Fair Labor Standards Act (FLSA), each job is classified as "exempt" or "non-exempt." This federal law establishes a minimum wage. It also provides standards for overtime pay, record keeping, and child labor. A job's duties, responsibilities, and compensation are considered when classifying jobs as exempt or non-exempt. A job should be classified as non-exempt, unless the job duties and responsibilities qualify the role as exempt under one of the specific exemptions defined in the FLSA (see FLSA Exemption Tests).

Employees in non-exempt jobs, usually hourly positions, are covered by the overtime provisions of the Act and must be paid overtime at time and one-half the regular hourly rate of pay for each hour worked over 40 hours per workweek. Some states, including California, require overtime pay for hours worked in excess of 8 hours per day. Jobs that are classified as exempt, usually salaried positions, are not subject to the overtime provision of the FLSA.

✓ Possible Starting Salary Offers

A salary range is identified for each job. Companies often offer three pay ranges: minimum, midpoint, and maximum. The specific starting salary that will be paid within that range is determined by considering salary expectation, work experience, knowledge, and skills of the person who will be performing the job. For example, an entry-level employee, who is just out of college with no work experience and little job knowledge and skills is usually paid at the lower end of the salary range. On the other hand, a skilled employee with years of work experience and an abundance of job knowledge and skills is usually paid at the higher end of the salary range or at least above midpoint. Also, the salaries of other employees performing that same or similar work along with budget and recruiting difficulty must be weighed when making salary decisions.

✓ Benefits of the Job

From health insurance to retirement plans, performance bonuses, education, paid time off and 401ks, benefits vary according to the organization. As the hiring manager, it is important that you are familiar with the benefits that your organization offers. Discuss the details of benefits offered for the job you are filling with your supervisor, compensation, benefits, or HR. Knowing this information will position you to answer most common benefit questions that candidates might have during and after the interview.

✓ Growth Opportunities (the "Will")

Determine what, if any, career paths exist for the job. Identify any probationary periods and approximate timelines for promotions and advancements, if applicable. Investigate what performance support (for example, coaching and mentoring) may be available to help the person hired to perform his or her job responsibilities. This is also a good place to identify how continuing education might be offered as performance support.

DETERMINE CULTURE FIT REQUIREMENTS

Organizational culture consists of traditions, attitudes, assumptions, values, rituals, routines—in short, culture is "how we do things around here." It is an invisible force that guides employees into compliance with the norms of the organization. After decades of research, professors Robert Quinn and Kim Cameron, from the University of Michigan, concluded that there are four types of organizational cultures. They are: **Collaborate, Create, Compete,** and **Control**—each with its own characteristics.

> **Collaborate-oriented cultures** are inclusive and focus on openness, team decision-making, and fostering a sense of belonging among its members ("doing things together").
>
> **Create-oriented cultures** embrace innovation and risk-taking and are often described as entrepreneurial and being on the cutting edge ("doing things first").
>
> **Compete-oriented cultures** are results-oriented, with a focus on competition, performance, and achieving goals ("doing things fast").
>
> **Control-oriented cultures** are structured and formal, with a focus on efficiency, dependability, and delivering with consistency ("doing things right").

Although culture has been described as "the glue that binds organizations together," employees find it difficult to work for a company when the culture is not consistent with their values and work behaviors. For example, within a three-month timespan, while writing this book, I had discussions with two senior-level colleagues who had recently started new jobs. Though hired for critical positions, they left their respective new organizations within six months of being hired. In both cases, they chose to leave because the culture of the organization was not consistent with their personal values and work behavior. In other words, they were not a good fit for the existing culture at these organizations. And at the senior level, it is an expensive endeavor to replace these employees, in terms of both dollars and credibility.

Most of us have worked with employees who were competent in their jobs but were not a good fit for the culture. In those instances, it was obvious that the hiring manager did not do his or her due diligence with regard to assessing culture fit requirements for the job and organization. So, in addition to identifying what work experience, education, and skill level are required for the position, you should explore how this position must function within the culture to determine what work behaviors will be required. Overlooking this important factor is neither helpful for the job candidates nor the organization, and will likely result in frustration, employee derailment, and unnecessary costs due to job turnover.

"As a business owner or manager, you know that hiring the wrong person is the most costly mistake you can make."
— Brian Tracy

The cost of replacing an employee due to turnover can be as much as 75% of his or her salary. For a manager earning an annual salary of $80,000, it could cost up to $60,000 to replace him or her. And the cost of replacing higher-level employees is even higher. In the end, hiring a candidate who is not a fit may cast a negative light on the incumbent and on you, the hiring manager, and it does both of you a great disservice when you get it wrong.

WRITE THE JOB ADVERTISEMENT

When writing the advertisement, create a profile of the job that looks not just at what you seek today, but what you desire for the future. I mentioned earlier that when you think of hiring the best-fit employee, you shouldn't think of it as a short-term endeavor. Therefore, when writing the advertisement, create a profile of the job with a minimum of a three-year view in mind.

Now that you have gathered all the important information about the job requirements, it's time to write the job advertisement. You might be used to the term "job announcement" to refer to a job vacancy posting. I use the word "advertisement" to specifically mean that it should be more than an announcement. Your advertisement should sell the position and directly target qualified candidates who are a fit for the job and organization. When writing the advertisement, use language that is descriptive and focuses on defining the parameters of the job.

Although HR usually completes this part of the process, some organizations leave this part of the process up to the hiring manager. If it is necessary for you to write a job advertisement, do not underestimate its importance. You should construct the job advertisement so that it describes the "Can," the "Will," and the "Fit" criteria you established earlier. In other words, the job advertisement should describe the specifics of the job, facts about the organization, and the work behaviors of the person who is the ideal fit for the job. Including the work behaviors of the ideal person in the job advertisement will increase the likelihood that applicants who are the right fit for the job will apply.

I have had an interest in human behavior for most of my adult life. As a result, it was logical for me to research the relationship between job advertisements and ideal candidate attraction as a topic for my doctoral dissertation. My investigation focused on determining whether using ideal person work behaviors in a job advertisement influenced applicants to apply for the job.

For this study, I developed and used three job advertisements, each describing a different ideal work behavior. First, here's the information that was given universally:

BUSINESS MANAGEMENT POSITIONS AVAILABLE

General Information: Company X invites applications for three management positions in such areas as: accounting, finance, information technology, marketing, human resources, consumer research, and general management. Company X is a 120-year-old consumer products company with 90% of its brands commanding first or second place in their markets with annual sales exceeding $5 billion.

About the Job: Position requirements for the available positions include performing the following managerial duties in your area of specialty: planning and overseeing work distribution, forecasting and managing budgets, overseeing the use of information systems, managing projects, and hiring, developing, and leading employees.

Application Procedures: To apply for the position, please send a letter of application and professional résumé to Company X, Director of Human Resources, C/O Main Street Journal, Box 72295, Irving, TX 75062.

Company X is an Equal Access/Equal Opportunity Employer.

Added to each job advertisement was a different description of the ideal candidate's work behaviors: one advertisement favored inclusion, another favored control, and yet another favored openness. The following statements were used in their respective cases:

Inclusion: "The ideal candidates for this position enjoy working with others as a member of a team, like helping others feel included as part of the team, like being in the middle of the action, have a desire to involve others in all facets of the operation, and are willing to recognize others for their achievement."

Control: "The ideal candidates for this position are take-charge individuals who enjoy working in a structured environment, have the desire to influence others, seek out difficult challenges, command respect for their authority, and make decisions quickly."

Openness: "The ideal candidates for this position are friendly and open with people, enjoy sharing their personal feelings with others, do not like to keep secrets, confide in their work colleagues, and desire to work in a conflict-free environment."

The research results showed that individuals who were high on inclusion were most attracted to the job depicting a person with inclusion-focused work behaviors. Identical effects occurred for the control and openness-focused work behaviors.

The findings of this research proved that including required work behaviors in job advertisements increases the likelihood of attracting the best-fit candidate. If someone else wrote the job advertisement, you should review it to at least ensure that it properly describes the job being filled and includes salient information about the organization. The job application should include information about the best-fit person's ideal work behaviors.

DEVELOP APPLICANT POOL

In order to hire the best-fit candidate, you must develop a strong and diverse pool of qualified applicants to interview to fill the position. Since building a pool of qualified applicants is the immediate goal, you should use every available source to find qualified applicants.

Posting the job advertisement across multiple sources will likely increase the number of qualified applicants who apply for the job.

There are a number of sources you can use to create an applicant pool. These sources include websites like Careerbuilder and Monster, professional organizations like the Association for Talent Development, employment agencies and social networks such as LinkedIn, traditional newspaper advertisements, employee referrals, and even walk-ins.

Employee referrals are a low-cost way to build an applicant pool. And research has shown that there are specific benefits (aside from low costs) to using employee referrals. Studies have indicated that workers who were hired through employee referrals stayed on the job longer than workers who were hired through advertisements, employment agencies, and walk-ins.

Social networks are another low-cost and effective way of building an applicant pool. When drawing from these sources, you should follow every lead you generate and reach out to your professional network to find qualified candidates.

Some of the online employment resources, employment agencies, and newspapers may be costly, compared to the other sources. So cast your net far and wide and use as many sources as your budget allows.

Again, this part of the process is usually managed by HR, but hiring managers can often influence the posting to ensure that the job is advertising to the right audiences and attracting those people to the applicant pool. This is especially critical for jobs that are in high demand and as a result, pose a challenge to attracting qualified applicants. Although HR commonly posts jobs on familiar, yet relevant job sites, boards, and other media, you may have to be creative and try reaching out in unfamiliar ways for high demand positions.

Screen Résumés

The next step in the preparation phase is to screen résumés. Résumés are typically screened first by HR. Many HR departments use a recruiting software system to screen résumés. Such systems are programmed to scan the résumés for key words and weed out unqualified applicants before anyone ever looks at them.

After the software's scan, HR traditionally conducts a phone screening with applicants whose résumés pass the initial screening phase. Sometimes, HR will ask the hiring manager to develop the questions for the phone screening. Afterwards, HR sends the résumés that pass the phone screening to the hiring manager. Upon receipt of the résumés, the hiring manager screens them again and identifies the final candidates he or she would like to interview.

In some organizations, the hiring manager may be required to conduct the entire résumé screening process without the assistance of HR.

What to Look For in a Résumé

First, look for the applicant's summary of skills and career objective when screening a résumé. A good summary will present the applicant's capabilities using the desired skills; a bad summary will read like regurgitated jargon. Determine if the skills presented are consistent with the job for which he or she has applied.

By now, you should have completed the skills, knowledge, and work behaviors section of the Hiring Workbook. Use the information from the workbook to screen the applicants' résumés. You should seek to find the candidate who can demonstrate the skills and knowledge required for the job in a real-world situation. For example, if clerical and office management skills are important for performing the job, look for those skills on the résumé. You will validate whether or not the candidate has these skills during the interview.

Sometimes the required work experience or education sections of the résumé may be misleading. For example, one résumé might read that the applicant "attended" City University, not that he or she graduated from City University and earned a degree. Review résumés carefully for such phrases. When you find them, be prepared to discuss and seek clarifications from the candidate during the interview.

A good résumé is organized, concise, neat, and polished. It should provide references or exhibit the willingness to provide them. If the applicant submits a cover letter with the résumé, he or she should provide additional information that highlights specific content within the résumé. A cover letter should also indicate that the applicant has conducted research about the organization and is interested in being a member of it. (In some cases, online application systems do not allow the job applicant to submit a cover letter; in those instances, no cover letter will be available to you.)

Résumé Types

There are two main types of résumés—chronological and functional—with variations of each type.

The chronological résumé is the most traditional; it starts with the current or most recent positions and works backward. Education is also presented in reverse chronological order, with the most recent educational accomplishment listed first. This type of résumé should have no unexplained time gaps and should clearly illustrate the skills, knowledge, and experience of the applicant. If you notice a time gap in the work experience of an applicant, check to see if he or she completed any education or skills training during this time. Applicants will often put the reason for any gaps on their cover letters, if they provide one. If a cover letter is not provided with the résumé, you should ask about any gaps in employment during the interview.

An applicant should not be discounted merely because there is a gap in his or her employment. With that said, be sure that he or she is current on any regulatory or industry-specific credentials, like CPR or other certifications. The purpose of a chronological résumé is to show that the applicant has built progressive work experience over time and is ready for the next step in his or her career.

On the following page, I've included a sample chronological résumé to illustrate those principles.

PAT JONES

345 Any Street – Hill Valley, GA 30001
(404) 555-0145, pat.jones@email.com

ADMINISTRATIVE ASSISTANT

An accomplished professional with 12 years of experience providing various levels of administrative support. Has the ability to synthesize excellent planning, organization, and execution with meticulous attention to detail and a strong work ethic to produce remarkable outcomes. Always demonstrates professionalism and discretion in confidential matters. A tenacious worker with highly developed interpersonal skills and the following business related expertise:

- General Office Management
- Computer Savvy
- Communication- Verbal and Written
- SharePoint Design
- Project Management
- Customer Service
- Database Creation and Management
- Scheduling

PROFESSIONAL EXPERIENCE

New Day Healthcare, Inc., Atlanta, GA

Administrative Assistant to the Vice President of Marketing   2008 - present

- Create professional-looking memos, letters, reports, and spreadsheets using Word and Excel
- Screen and direct phone calls, take accurate messages, and ensure prompt delivery
- Retrieve and distribute a high volume of mail to the correct recipients
- Sensitively handle confidential information
- Schedule and maintain calendar of appointments (using Outlook), meetings, and travel arrangements—both through telephone and online bookings
- Handle competing priorities and tight deadlines—known for quality, timely completion of projects
- Assist with corporate tradeshows and events—from set-up to greeting guests

ABC Manufacturing, Atlanta, GA

Administrative Assistant to the Plant Manager   2002 - 2008

- Assisted Plant Manager in highly visible support role in a small, start-up company requiring daily customer contact
- Produced professional-looking correspondence and committee minutes using MS Word
- Used Word and Excel to create and update departmental processes
- Developed and maintained company-wide record keeping, data retention, and backup procedures
- Tactfully handled confidential information
- Oversaw quality control of procedures for entire organization
- Coordinated and organized multiple projects while completing them efficiently

EDUCATION & AFFILIATIONS

AAS, Business Administration with specialization in Office Management – University of Lifelong Learning

American Society of Administrative Professionals

REFERENCES

Provided upon request

Next, let's discuss the functional résumé. This type of résumé presents skills gained from a variety of work experiences as skill categories (for example, Business Acumen, Communication, Leadership and Teamwork). Each skill category has a heading followed by a description of the relevant work experience for that skill category. The actual job titles and dates of the work experiences are listed in reverse chronological order under a separate category at the top or bottom of the résumé. Educational accomplishments are also presented on this type of résumé.

The functional résumé may be used by applicants with little work experience, or those who possess a diverse set of skills and experience (for example, a recent college graduate, or a person who has had short tenures in multiple positions). On the other hand, it may be used by a person who has a lengthy work history, who chooses only the relevant highlights of his or her vast experience.

On the following page, I've included a sample functional résumé:

SAM SMITH

4321 Main Street, Hill Valley, GA 30001 ♦ 404.555.0113 ♦ sam.smith@email.com

A personable business professional with 10 years of experience providing customer service and administrative support. Experienced at setting up and maintaining customized SharePoint sites. Well versed in all applications of Microsoft Office. A "people person" who enjoys working on a team. Discreet in sensitive and confidential matters. Demonstrated history of producing accurate budgets and financial reports. Other related expertise includes:

• Logistics	• Public speaking	• Crisis Management Skills	• Grant writing
• Project management	• Book Keeping & Database Management	• Customer Relationship Management	• Event Planning

PROFESSIONAL EXPERIENCE

Communication and Customer Service

- Prepare complex letters, memos, reports, Excel spreadsheets, and other correspondence
- Greet walk-in customers, assess their needs and provide unparalleled customer service
- Communicate product knowledge to customers using layman's terms to facilitate understanding

Planning and Organizing

- Schedule meetings and coordinate transportation, flight, and hotel reservations
- Planned and coordinated global meetings with clients in Mexico, Asia, and Australia
- Maintained procurement account for the department—utilized MS Excel to develop a supply inventory using a first-in-first-out technique to ensure that products were used before expiry date

Technology and Problem Solving

- Developed and managed team SharePoint site
- Used MS Outlook to prioritize and track task completion. Used Skype, WebEx, MS Lync and GoToMeeting to schedule client and vendor interviews. Troubleshot connection issues.
- Used Google Analytics to track company website usage and coordinated the development of a software application to increase the volume of visitors to the website

EMPLOYMENT HISTORY

Maxwell Wellness Center – Hill Valley, GA
Administrative Assistant to the President, 2008 to Present

Aaron Manufacturing – Sandy Springs, GA
Administrative Assistant to the Plant Manager, 2006 to 2008

Hill Valley Restaurant & Café – Hill Valley, GA
Waitress, 2004 to 2006

EDUCATION

BS Degree, Office Management – Hill Valley University – 2006

AFFILIATIONS

International Association of Administrative Professionals (IAAP)

REFERENCES

Provided upon request

DEVELOP INTERVIEW QUESTIONS

The next step in the hiring process is to develop questions for the interview. Remember our discussion earlier about using a structured process to hire? What were the three criteria we discussed that will yield best-fit candidates? (The "Can," the "Will," and the "Fit.")

Use the factors below to create the interview questions. Doing so will help you determine if the candidate meets the three requirements:

The "Can"	The "Will"	The "Fit"
Skills	Likes	Style
Knowledge	Motivations	Personality
Education	References	Work Behavior
Experience	Career Objectives	Job & Company

Can the candidate do the job?

At this point, you have spent a significant amount of time identifying the knowledge and skills requirements for the job. Developing questions, such as the examples given below, will help you determine if the candidate possesses the required skills and knowledge:

✓ "Describe your experience with Microsoft Excel. Explain your approach to entering and maintaining information in spreadsheets using this software. What were the results of using this approach?"

✓ "Tell me about your experience with SharePoint. How have you used it to set up and manage workflows, metrics reporting and other tasks? How did your method of using this system impact the organization?"

✓ "Describe the skills that you have relied on most to be successful. How have you used them during your career and what has been their impact?"

✓ "Tell me about a time when you did not have the skills required to perform a job successfully. What skills were you lacking? What actions did you take to resolve your skills deficit? What were the results?"

Will the candidate do the job?

These questions relate directly to what motivates the candidate. Examples of questions that will help you determine what drives the candidate to perform well are:

✓ "What are your career goals? What are you doing to achieve them? In what way will this job contribute to you achieving them?"
✓ "There are times when we work without close supervision or support to get the job done. Tell me about a time when you found yourself in such a situation. How did things turn out?"
✓ "Which aspects of the job you are interviewing for today energize you? On the flip side, which parts are least likely to be your favorite?"
✓ "What is the most challenging part of your current/most recent job? How do you overcome this challenge?"

Is the candidate a good Fit for the job?

Remember our discussion about work behaviors as the "it" factor(s)? As I mentioned before, they're important and they often get overlooked during the interview. Examples of questions to determine fit for the job (as well as the culture within the organization) include:

✓ "Describe an important project you worked on with team members who had different work styles from you. How did you handle the differences and what was the outcome?"
✓ "Recall a work situation in which you felt that your values

might be compromised. How did you work through the situation and what was the outcome?"

✓ "Tell me about a time when you were under stress on the job. How did you work through it and what resulted from your actions?"

✓ "Do you prefer to work on a team or as an individual contributor? Tell me about a time when you had to function in a least preferred role. What was the situation? How did it turn out?"

Question Types and Techniques

The questions presented in the previous section don't lend themselves to yes-or-no, one-word responses. The reason for that is all of the questions above are behavior-based questions. Although other types of questions are used during interviews, this book focuses primarily on behavior-based questions. Why?

A well-written behavior-based question will prompt the candidate to explain and discuss his or her answers, as opposed to inviting a simple "yes" or "no" response. Research studies have consistently shown that behavior-based questions are more effective at predicting job success than other types of questions (almost six times more effective). This is because behavior-based questions are effective at eliciting information from a candidate about his or her job skills, knowledge, and performance. I'll discuss more about behavior-based questions and other types of questions next.

About Behavior-Based Questions

From the examples above, how would you define behavior-based questions? Behavior-based questions are used to obtain specific examples of a candidate's past actions; the strength of these questions is based on the fact that past behaviors are the best predictors of future behaviors.

Among different methods of interviewing, most non-HR hiring managers find that using behavior-based questions is the easiest yet most effective way to predict the future job success of candidates they interview. This is because using behavior-based questioning techniques does not require as much experience as some of the other questioning techniques to use effectively.

With behavior-based interviewing, the candidate is asked to provide information on a defined situation. The candidate is also asked to explain how he or she reacted to the situation and to describe the outcome as a result of the action(s) that he or she took. This is often referred to as the SAR approach, or Situation-Action-Result.

Using the SAR Approach

Think of the acronym SAR (Situation-Action-Result) when you develop your behavior-based questions.

Here are two examples of behavior-based question series that use the SAR approach:

Example 1
"Tell me about a situation in which you had to adjust to changes over which you had no control." (Situation)
"How did you manage?" (Action)
"How did it turn out?" (Result)

Example 2
"What do you do when priorities change quickly?" (Action)
"Give an example of when this occurred." (Situation)
"What happened as a result?" (Result)

Here are some additional examples of behavior-based questions. Use them and the SAR acronym as guidelines for developing your own behavior-based questions.

✓   "Describe a problem you solved that required looking beyond the obvious. What was the outcome?"

✓   "Tell me more about your problem-solving skills. You stated that problem solving is one of your strengths. Give me at least three examples of how you used it as a strength in the past. Explain the results for each example."

✓   "We are asking for proficiency in Excel, so we need a real spreadsheet wizard. Describe for me the most complex documentation you have had to create in Excel and what it was used for."

✓   "Your résumé states you have excellent interpersonal skills. Tell me about your relationships with your current manager, a colleague, and someone who works on another team. Do you perceive them as a challenge to work with? Describe how you interact with them to get work accomplished."

✓   "Tell me about a time when you had to present complex information. How did you ensure that the other person understood? What was the result?"

✓   "What do you do when your schedule is interrupted? Give an example of how you handle it."

✓   "Give me an example of a situation that required you to go above and beyond your job description. What actions did you take? What difference did your actions make?"

✓   "Tell me about a time when you built a positive working relationship with someone under difficult conditions. How did it turn out?"

Situational Questions

Situational questions are another type of questioning approach. Situational questions are based on hypothetical scenarios. These questions are used to prompt the candidate to explain what he or she would do in a hypothetical situation.

For example, a candidate for an administrative assistant position might be asked: "Explain how you would handle an irate caller on the phone." Hypothetical questions like this are beneficial for learning about a candidate's work behavior—especially his or her interpersonal skills, in this case. Here are other examples of situational questions:

✓ "A co-worker tells you in confidence that he needs some personal time off to attend an important parent/teacher meeting at his child's school, but he has no vacation left. He informs you that he plans to call in sick tomorrow so he can attend the meeting. What would you do and why?"

✓ "You have been working hard over the last six months to identify a solution to a problem your team is having. You just came up with what you believe to be a solid solution to the problem and presented it to the team. Their reaction was not what you expected. Instead of excitedly congratulating you for a great solution and a job well done, they shot down your recommendation. Explain how you would handle your team's reaction to your recommendation."

Open-Ended and Closed-Ended Questions

You will likely use open-ended questions (that are not behavior-based) and closed-ended questions during an interview. Examples of the appropriate use of each type of question are presented in the second slice (Interview) in this book. For now, let's focus on what you need to know when developing these questions.

Open-ended questions encourage a candidate to respond with detailed information. They are questions that begin as follows:

> What . . .
> Why . . .
> How . . .
> Tell me . . .
> Describe . . .
> Explain . . .

These types of questions are useful for inquiring about a candidate's qualifications and for following-up on his or her response to a previous question. Below are examples of open-ended questions.

- ✓ "What steps or method do you use to solve problems?"
- ✓ "How did you develop the required skills for this job?"
- ✓ "Explain your approach to working with employees whose work styles are different from yours."

Closed-ended questions only require a "yes" or "no" response from a candidate, so they should be used sparingly. They are questions that begin as follows:

> Is . . .
> Did . . .
> Do . . .
> Could . . .
> Would . . .
> Will . . .

These types of questions are useful for managing the interview (for example, when a candidate strays off course). The following are examples of closed-ended questions:

- ✓ "Is problem-solving one of your strengths?"
- ✓ "Do you have the required skills for this job?"

✓   "Would you be able to work with employees whose work styles are different from yours?"

Concerns about Asking Improper Questions

Earlier in the book, I mentioned that the hiring process should be structured and that the candidate selection tools (such as the interview process, questions and evaluation forms) are governed by the same guidelines as a competency test. Let's explore those statements in greater detail now.

Over the years, I have conducted a plethora of workshops on hiring practices. I usually start the sessions with an activity. I divide the participants into two groups: the job candidate group and the hiring manager group. Then, I ask each group to brainstorm and list the concerns they have had when preparing for interviews as either candidates or hiring managers. In all the years I have used this activity, without fail, the hiring manager group has always written a concern about asking inappropriate or illegal questions during the interview. To me, this illustrates that there are far too many managers conducting interviews and hiring job candidates without a good knowledge of local, state and federal guidelines.

Once I had a senior leader approach me after a workshop. He said: "I have a problem with female employees quitting after being hired." He then went on to ask: "How do I find out if they plan to have children before I hire them? How can I legally ask them that question? It's a real problem for me."

I told him that the question is unlawful. Federal law requires that hiring decisions be based solely on the candidate's job qualifications; a woman's current or future pregnancy plans are not relevant to her qualifications. I gave him my best advice: if the question does not relate to the job, don't ask it.

The Legality of Interview Questions

Hiring practices must be lawful to be effective. Therefore, during the development of the interview questions and during the actual interview, you should ensure that the questions adhere to federal laws regarding employment discrimination.

Court rulings and the U.S. Equal Employment Opportunity Commission (EEOC) have prohibited hiring practices (such as job applications and interview questions) that disproportionately screen out applicants based on their race, color, religion, sex (including pregnancy), national origin, age (40 or over), disability or genetic information. Individuals who fall within these categories are members of a "protected class," as defined by federal law.

Appropriate interview questions should not elicit information about any protected class. Appropriate questions should focus on the candidate's skills, knowledge, experience, and work behavior as they relate to the job for which he or she has applied. Your questions will likely be considered inappropriate by the job candidate—and may be illegal—if they are unrelated to his or her qualifications and do not assess ability to perform the job. Asking inappropriate questions during the hiring process could form the basis for a discrimination claim against your organization.

Before writing interview questions, let's take a closer look at what makes a question inappropriate. I've provided some examples below of inappropriate questions (as sorted by the protected-class factors we just discussed), along with explanations for why the questions are legally inappropriate and some appropriate questions you might ask instead.

Many of these explanations about the inappropriate questions were taken directly from the Equal Employment Opportunity Commission (EEOC) website (www.EEOC.gov) with minor editing to make the text consistent with the format of this book.

Race or Color

INAPPROPRIATE—What race are you? Are you a minority? What is your natural hair color?

WHY—According to the EEOC, employers should not inquire about a candidate's race unless there is a legitimate business need for such information (i.e., tracking affirmative action data). If an employer has such a need, the information should be kept separate from the other hiring documents and the employer must guard against using it in a discriminatory manner. Asking for race-related information on the telephone is never justified.

APPROPRIATE—Unless there is a legitimate business need, it is not appropriate to inquire about race or color.

Height & Weight

INAPPROPRIATE—How much do you weigh? Have you ever been overweight? How tall are you?

WHY—Height and weight requirements tend to disproportionately limit the employment opportunities of some protected groups. Unless the employer can demonstrate how the need is related to the job, it may be viewed as illegal. A number of states and localities have laws prohibiting discrimination on the basis of height and weight unless these are job-related requirements. Inquiries about height and weight should be avoided unless they are job-related.

APPROPRIATE—Unless job-related, it is not appropriate to inquire about height and weight.

Credit Rating or Economic Status

INAPPROPRIATE—Do you own your home or do you rent? Do you own a car? Have you ever overdrawn your checking account?

WHY—Inquiry into an applicant's current or past assets, liabilities, or credit rating, including bankruptcy or garnishment, refusal or cancellation of bonding, car ownership, rental or ownership of a house, length of residence at an address, charge accounts, furniture ownership, or bank accounts generally should be avoided because they tend to impact more adversely on minorities and females. Exceptions exist if the employer can show that such information is essential to the particular job in question. An increasing number of states specifically prohibit these inquiries except in very limited circumstances.

APPROPRIATE—Unless the candidate's credit rating and economic status is essential to the job, it is not appropriate to inquire about them.

Religious Affiliation or Beliefs

INAPPROPRIATE—What is your religious affiliation? Are you a member of a parish or church? What holidays do you observe? Will your religion prevent you from working weekends or holidays?

WHY—The above questions are inappropriate and are generally viewed as non-job-related and legally problematic. The only exception is if the religion is a bona fide occupational qualification (BFOQ). According to the EEOC, employers whose purpose and character is primarily religious (for example, religious corporations, associations, educational institutions, or societies) are exempt from this law and are permitted to lean towards hiring persons of the same religion. The burden is on the employer to claim this exemption and demonstrate that they qualify.

APPROPRIATE—Unless the religion-related question is a BFOQ, it is not appropriate to inquire about religious affiliation or beliefs.

Citizenship

INAPPROPRIATE—Where were you born? Are you a United States citizen? In what country were your parents born?

WHY—The above questions can be the basis for discrimination based on national origin. The EEOC guidelines protect both citizens and non-citizens who reside in the US against discrimination based on national origin. Except in the interest of national security, a candidate who is legally eligible to work in the US may not be discriminated against on the basis of his or her citizenship.

APPROPRIATE—Are you legally authorized to work in the United States?

Marital Status & Children

INAPPROPRIATE—Are you married? Are you pregnant? Do you have children or plan to have children in the future? What are the ages of your children? What are your childcare arrangements? Will your parenting responsibility interfere with your work responsibility?

WHY—Questions regarding marital status and children are gender-biased and are frequently used to discriminate against female candidates. According to Title VII of the Civil Rights Act, it is unlawful to deny a female candidate a job because of her marital status, if she has children, or if she is planning to have children in the future.

APPROPRIATE—There are no appropriate questions about marital status and children.

Age

INAPPROPRIATE—How old are you? What is your birthday? In what year were you born? When did you graduate from high school? How do you feel about having a young supervisor?

WHY—The Age Discrimination in Employment Act (ADEA) prohibits questions about age as this may deter older candidates from applying for a job. Candidates and employees who are age 40 or over are protected from discrimination under the Act. An employer may inquire about the age of candidates only in those very rare situations where age is a bona fide occupational qualification (BFOQ). For example, because of the mandatory retirement requirements for pilots, a hiring manager at an airline company may inquire about the age of an applicant applying for a job as a pilot.

APPROPRIATE—Unless age is a BFOQ (which it probably is not), limit age-related questions to "Are you 18 years of age or older? If hired, can you provide proof of your age?"

Gender

INAPPROPRIATE—What is your gender preference? Does your spouse object to you working overtime or traveling? Who will care for your children when you work overtime or travel?

WHY—These questions are inappropriate because they are gender-biased and discriminatory towards female candidates. According to the EEOC, questions about a candidate's sex, (unless it is BFOQ and is essential to a particular position or occupation), marital status, pregnancy, medical history of pregnancy, future child-bearing plans, number and/or ages of children or dependents, provisions for child care, abortions, birth control, ability to reproduce, and name or address of spouse or children are generally viewed as non-job-related and problematic under Title VII.

APPROPRIATE—Can you meet the work requirements for the job? What hours can you work? Can you work on weekends and holidays (if weekend or holiday work is required for the job being applied for)?

Arrest & Conviction

INAPPROPRIATE—Have you ever been arrested?

WHY—According to EEOC guidelines, asking candidates about their arrest record is inappropriate. A potential employer can, however, ask candidates if they have any criminal convictions, if job-related. Even so, some state laws require employers to wait until late in the hiring process to ask about conviction records.

APPROPRIATE—Have you ever been convicted of a crime? If so when, where, and what was the disposition of the case? (Legal counsel should be consulted before making any decision not to hire based on candidates' conviction record.)

Disabilities

INAPPROPRIATE—What is the nature of your disabilities? Have you ever received worker's compensation? How many sick days have you taken this year in your current job?

WHY—Employers generally cannot ask disability-related questions or require medical examinations until after a candidate has been given a conditional job offer. Employers may ask limited questions about reasonable accommodation, if they reasonably believe that the candidate may need accommodation because of an obvious or voluntarily disclosed disability, or where the candidate has disclosed a need for accommodation.

According to the Americans with Disabilities Act (ADA), an employer cannot legally ask a candidate if he or she has a specific disability. An employer is also prohibited from asking candidates any question that may reveal information about a disability.

APPROPRIATE—Can you perform the duties of the job you are applying for with or without accommodation?

Medical Questions & Examinations

INAPPROPRIATE—Do you have any chronic medical conditions? Are you currently taking any prescription medications? Were any problems found during your last physical examination? Are you willing to take a medical examination before your second interview?

WHY—Under the Americans with Disabilities Act (ADA), an employer may not ask a job candidate to answer medical questions or take a medical exam before making a job offer. An employer may ask candidates whether they can perform the job and how they would perform the job. The law allows an employer to condition a job offer on the candidate answering certain medical questions or successfully passing a medical exam, but only if all new employees in the same job have to answer the questions or take the exam and they are job-related.

APPROPRIATE—Can you perform the duties of the job you are applying for with or without accommodation? Explain how you would load a customer's order on the truck.

The questions in the above sets are not meant to be an exhaustive list of appropriate and inappropriate questions. They are provided to familiarize you with the major laws and guidelines governing interview questions. As you develop your own interview questions, use the information presented to guide the formulation of your questions. A quick reference guide containing an additional list of appropriate and inappropriate questions is presented in the second slice (Interview) of this book. Additional information can also be found at the EEOC website (www.EEOC.gov).

PLAN THE INTERVIEW

The next step of the preparation phase is planning the interview itself. Several questions must be answered before you can plan the interview:

- ✓ Will the interview be conducted one-on-one with the candidate or will it be conducted as a panel?
- ✓ If conducted as a panel, which questions or areas will each panelist cover?
- ✓ Will a follow-up interview be necessary? If so, will the panelists be involved in the follow-up phase?

---

*"You need to have a **collaborative** hiring process."*
— Steve Jobs

Involve Team Members

Since people collaborate in the workplace to accomplish work effectively, it is a good practice to involve other team members in the interviewing process. And when you are close to making an offer, you might want to include your boss in the process as well. Team members' involvement may include taking part in the formal interview, or taking the candidate to lunch or dinner. Feedback from team members about the time they spent with the candidate often provides invaluable information that may be helpful in determining if the candidate is a fit for the culture. Inform team members in advance that you will consider their feedback when making the final hiring decision.

However, as the hiring manager, the ultimate decision and account-ability for hiring the best-fit candidate resides with you. This is why guidelines are extremely important when inviting others to join the interview process.

While hiring for the "Can," the "Will," and the "Fit," your team members and your boss will have their own perspective of the candidate. This makes for a richer evaluation of the candidate and is more likely to result in a best-fit candidate. You also get the benefit of buy-in from others, since inclusion allows everyone to be invested in making the result a successful hire.

Make Sure Team Members Keep It Legal

There is an important caution, however, when having team members participate in the interview: keep it legal! Whether taking part in the formal interview or just going to lunch with the candidate, team members must ensure that they do not stray off the "legal turf." They should keep discussions appropriate at all times. I have learned from experience that even experienced hiring managers are capable of straying away from the "legal turf."

On one occasion, an internal candidate traveled to our Chicago office for a final interview. Our company was considering this candidate for a lead role in our West coast operations. The candidate had been an excellent employee, had worked with the company for several years, and had an all-around solid track record. The interview wrapped up around 5:30 p.m., and we extended a job offer on the spot. The candidate did not immediately accept the offer, so the hiring manager and I decided to continue discussing the job and its requirements with the candidate over dinner.

Dinner went well. We discussed more details about the specific role the candidate would perform. As we provided more information about the job's travel requirements, we learned that the candidate was apprehensive about flying. For no apparent reason, the hiring manager leaned in towards the candidate, as if he was going to say something profound, and said: "What you need to do is discuss this job and its travel requirements with your husband."

Yikes! You guessed it—the candidate was a woman, and the hiring manager had just violated both EEOC pre-hire guidelines and our own company policy by saying that. I spent the remaining time at dinner apologizing to the candidate and un-doing the damaging comment made by the hiring manager. I assured her that it was not the company's policy or my expectation, as the lead staffing person, to require her to consult with anyone about the job offer we had extended to her.

In addition to the unlawfulness of the statement made by the hiring manager, this was, without a doubt, one of the most embarrassing moments of my professional career.

A word to the wise: make sure everyone who will be involved in the interview process keeps the conversation appropriate and legal at all times. As the hiring manager, you must ensure that those invited to participate in the interview understand its burdens and responsibilities.

Selecting the Interview Design and Method

Companies typically interview candidates face-to-face or virtually; sometimes both methods are used. When deciding which interview method to use, keep in mind that each method has advantages and disadvantages.

Interviewing face-to-face allows the interviewer to observe the nonverbal cues of the candidate. It minimizes distractions and makes it easier for the candidate to remain focused on the interviewer and on answering the questions.

The virtual interviewing platform offers cost-effective interviewing options by using recorded video ("asynchronous") or live video ("synchronous") interview methods. This option provides flexibility for the candidate and the interviewer. If a recorded video interview is used, pre-recorded questions are sent to the candidate. The candidate is instructed to record his or her response to the questions on video and return them by a certain date. The candidate's recorded responses can be shared with others, like department members who could provide feedback to help make the final hiring decision.

As the hiring manager, you will need to decide whether to conduct a face-to-face interview, a virtual interview, or both.

Once you have decided on the interview design and method and secured your panelists (if using any), you are ready to plan the interview session. Start by developing a functional agenda, then build on it. A typical interview agenda may consist of the following components:

Topic	Time
Introductions	5 Minutes
Work Experience, Motivation, and Fit	35 Minutes
Education, Training, Other Job-Related Info	10 Minutes
Summary, Questions & Closing	10 Minutes

An interview usually lasts about an hour but could last longer, depending on the level of the position. The above agenda is typical and will vary depending on level of the job and candidates. As part of the planning process, you must also attend to other related tasks:

Additional Tasks to Plan

✓ *Coordinate interview date and time.* Whether interviewing the candidate one-on-one or as part of a panel, the date and time of the interview should be coordinated with everyone involved as soon as possible. In many organizations, HR coordinates the interview. If this task becomes your responsibility, taking care of it sooner rather than later will provide maximum planning time for everyone.

✓ *Reserve a private space.* If you have a private office that is adequate for conducting an interview, great; you can conduct the interview there. If not, locate and schedule an adequate interview space. By "adequate," I mean a private area that allows for an intimate discussion, preferably a round table, if possible. Remember, the space will help set the tone for the interview, so make it positive and comfortable.

✓ *Arrange the chairs.* If a round table is not available, consider conducting the interview without a table or desk. In this case, you should arrange the chairs to create a power-neutral environment which fosters an intimate discussion. If you must interview at your desk, consider placing the chair, where the candidate will sit, beside your desk instead of in front of it. This arrangement will also create more of a power-neutral situation.

✓ *Conduct a virtual trial run.* If the candidate will be interviewed from a remote location, then make arrangements to do a trial run of the technology prior to the actual interview.

✓ *Forward or send phones to voicemail.* The phone ringing in the middle of an interview is not professional and is not likely to make a good impression on the candidate. In addition to forwarding or sending your office phone to voicemail, make sure your cell phone is silenced. In fact, it is best to place your cell phone in a desk drawer so it is does not cause distraction. Silence your computer notifications as well. And, if you are experiencing an emergency and you predict an interruption may occur, be sure to let the candidate know at the beginning of the interview to lessen the impact if it occurs.

✓ *Clear your desk.* Even if you don't plan to conduct the interview at your desk, make sure it is clean and tidy along with the rest of the interview space. Remember that the candidate is mea-suring you up, not simply the other way around. Conducting the interview in an organized space will contribute to making a positive impression on the candidate. Ensure that all confidential information (such as other candidates' resumes, pricing information, client information, staff information, trade secrets, and agreements) is put away and is not within view of the candidate.

✓ *Clear your mind.* Keeping a clear mind would be easy to do if your only job responsibility nowadays were to hire a good candidate. However, if you are like most hiring managers, you will still have to perform your regular duties while interviewing. One simple yet effective method that I use to keep a clear mind during the interview is to make a to-do list for after the interview. This allows me to manage my time and remain focused during the interview. If you don't have a clear mind, it will show during the interview. This reflects poorly on you and the organization.

✓ *Practice.* Now that the other planning tasks are completed, it is time to practice. Yes, you should actually rehearse the interview. Practice helps get the timing of the interview right, so you can keep pace and set enough time aside to gather the right information. Practice also helps you not feel rushed.

As is the case with other preparation phases, preparing to hire is time-consuming, especially for busy managers. The good news is that you do not have to complete all of the preparation at one time. You can spread the tasks out over time to pace yourself, as time allows. Delegating some of the tasks to others, such as developing and reviewing interview questions, is another way to lighten your work load. (Of course, if you choose to delegate that, ensure you review the questions to ensure their validity and legality before the interview begins.) Whatever method you choose for getting it done, taking the time to make a solid plan for the interview, and then practicing it, will be well worth the effort in the end.

The Second Slice—INTERVIEW

After reviewing the résumés, you will likely end up with a few applicants that you would consider advancing to the next stage in the process. An "applicant" becomes a "candidate" when he or she advances to the next stage of the hiring process: the interview.

So you have mulled over the résumés that you have reviewed and you have identified the candidates that you would like to interview. The interview appointments have been scheduled. You have adequately prepared for this moment, using the preparation tips from the first slice of this book. You are ready to select the best-fit candidate!

What Exactly is a Job Interview?
To be an effective interviewer, it is important to understand what an interview is and is not. A job interview is an interactive discussion between a potential employer—the interviewer—and a job candidate. In other words, an interview is a dialogue, not a monologue. It is a qualitative approach to gathering information that can be described as "a conversation with a purpose."

In a job interview, the purpose of the conversation is to obtain the information required to answer three questions about a candidate:

1. Does the candidate have the ability to do the job? (the "Can")
2. Is the candidate motivated to do the job? (the "Will")
3. Is the candidate a fit for the organization? (the "Fit")

Although an interview primarily consists of a question-and-answer exchange with the job candidate, it is not meant to be one-way;

rather, an interview should show real interaction between the interviewer and job candidate. This two-way exchange is likely to make a
more positive impression on the candidate than a one-way question
and answer session. The reality is that, while you are evaluating the
candidate, the candidate is taking note of your appearance, behavior,
knowledge, and motivation as an interviewer. Candidates routinely
use their impressions of the interviewer to form an opinion of you
and the organization.

When done properly, the interview will result in increasing the likelihood of hiring the best candidate, thus decreasing turnover and hiring
costs. It will also promote and improve the image of the company.
And, since you'll be doing it properly (right?), you'll be ensuring that
your company is compliant with applicable employment laws (local,
state, and federal).

To conduct an effective interview, you must be familiar with a few
key interviewing tasks. Performing these tasks well will allow you to
manage the interview, while gathering the information necessary to
make the right hiring decision. The tasks include the following:

- ☐ **Open the Interview**
- ☐ **Conduct the Interview**
- ☐ **Close the Interview**

OPEN THE INTERVIEW

As with anything, the manner in which an interview is opened
sets the tone for what follows. The hiring manager should display
confidence and professionalism the moment he or she meets the
candidate. This will help to establish a positive tone, which should be
consistent throughout the interview. Maintaining a positive environment
provides a pleasant interviewing experience for both the candidate
and the interviewer.

Build Rapport

Most of us know what it is like to really connect with someone we've just met. When it happens, there is a feeling of harmony and accordance with the new person within a very short time of meeting. Perhaps this is "rapport."

"Rapport is the ability to enter someone else's world, to make him feel that you understand him, that you have a strong common bond."
— Tony Robbins

Knowing how to build rapport with others is key to success in any given interaction. Rapport can be described as mutual trust and emotional affinity that someone has with another person or a group. Building rapport during an interview fosters an open environment and helps the candidate feel at ease, thereby bringing out his or her best nature. When a candidate is at ease, he or she is more likely to be open with you and to share more valuable information during the interview.

As soon as you meet the candidate, you should begin to establish rapport. Using the candidate's name, making friendly small talk, and showing empathy towards him or her as a job seeker will go a long way to help build rapport. Examples of comments that will help you build rapport with the candidate (without straying off the legal turf) are:

- ✓ "Did you have trouble finding our office?"
- ✓ "I'm looking forward to learning more about your work experience and skills."
- ✓ "If you don't understand any of my questions, please don't hesitate to ask for clarity."

✓   "Are you doing OK?"
✓   "Thank you."

Using friendly nonverbal cues is also helpful for building rapport. The interviewer's body language plays an important role in building and maintaining rapport through nonverbal means. These nonverbal cues include:

✓   Shaking hands firmly
✓   Maintaining eye contact
✓   Maintaining good posture but leaning in, when appropriate
✓   Giving the candidate your undivided attention
✓   Nodding and smiling, when appropriate

Mention Your Note-Taking

Once you have set rapport-building in motion, tell the candidate that you will be taking notes during the interview and explain why. A common explanation is that you are interviewing several candidates and you don't want to forget any of his or her responses to your questions.

Taking notes does not mean writing down everything the candidate says verbatim. It means capturing key words and phrases to summarize the candidate's responses to your questions. Be sure to maintain eye contact with the candidate periodically while taking notes in order to maintain rapport. Don't let the note-taking interfere with the flow of the interview; try to take notes as unobtrusively as possible.

Promote the Company

In addition to building rapport and explaining why you are taking notes, you should conduct yourself professionally throughout the interview. Presenting a friendly and positive image and showing interest in the candidate's career goals, help to promote the company and the position for which the candidate is interviewing. Research shows that the interviewer's professionalism, friendliness, and interest in the candidate significantly and positively influence candidates' image of the organization and attraction to the job.

Maintaining eye contact with the candidate, listening actively, nodding, and smiling are examples of interviewer friendliness. The interviewer's behavior and personality (warmth, supportiveness, competence, enthusiasm, interest in the candidate, etc.), along with the professional manner in which the interview is conducted, are the most consistent positive influences on organizational image and job attraction. Providing the candidate with information about the company and its affiliates will also contribute to building a positive image of the company. Interviewers should be prepared to provide company-specific information to the candidates during the interview.

CONDUCT THE INTERVIEW

Now it is time to have that "conversation with a purpose." Remember, the purpose of this conversation is to determine if the candidate meets the requirements for the job (the "Can," the "Will," and the "Fit"). To accomplish this, you need to leverage the candidate's and your own interpersonal skills to create and maintain an effective dialogue throughout the interview.

Ask and Respond to Questions

Preparations you made during the previous PREPARE phase—tasks like writing good behavior-based questions in advance—should position you well to question candidates effectively to obtain job-specific information. As an interviewer, asking questions is the primary means by which you have to determine if a candidate is the best qualified for the job. Your approach to asking questions during the interview should be one of having a back-and-forth behavior-based conversation with the candidate.

Watch Out for Telegraphing

When asking a candidate non-behavior-based questions, you should make every effort not to telegraph the correct response to him or her. Telegraphing occurs when an interviewer asks a candidate a question in a way that suggests what the correct answer should be. For example:

- ✓ "We need someone in this position who has excellent interpersonal skills. How are your interpersonal skills?"
- ✓ "We value initiative around here. How would you describe your initiative?"

In the examples above, the candidate could easily perceive what response the interviewer is looking for and would likely provide that response. Telegraphing during a non-behavior-based interview will usually cause candidates to distort how good a fit they are for the position.

Include Behavior-Based Questions

I mentioned earlier that behavior-based questions are better than other question types. One of the reasons is that they minimize the risk of telegraphing. To the extent that telegraphing occurs in behavior-based interviewing, it is more difficult for the candidate to fabricate a response (and to maintain any fabrications) throughout the interview. This is because behavior-based questions solicit factual and descriptive examples, not hypothetical ones. The candidate is required to provide solid evidence to support his or her claim of skills, experience, motivation, or fit. Using an array of behavior-based questions makes it unlikely that the candidate will remember how he or she responded earlier, which makes it difficult to maintain less-than-accurate responses.

Not only is it difficult for a candidate to maintain any fabrications when asked behavior-based questions, but these types of questions are also more predictive of the candidate's future job performance, compared to other types of questions. To the interviewer, asking behavior-based questions is like watching a movie of the candidate replaying how he or she has used the required skills, knowledge and work behavior to handle past situations. Remember to use the Situation–Action–Results (SAR) acronym presented in the first slice of PIE, PREPARE, as a guide for formulating and asking behavior-based questions.

Sometimes candidates will become overwhelmed with the multilayered behavior-based questions and may forget to answer all the components of the question. Candidates may ask you to repeat the question to ensure they have answered all the components; do so willingly or assure them that they have answered the question completely. If there are gaps in the responses, there are techniques you can use to get any missing information you need. We will discuss those techniques next.

Probe for Job-Related Specifics

While you should make every effort to ask behavior-based questions, you will sometimes find it necessary to ask specific probing questions to dig deeper to gather the information you need from the candidate. For example, you may need to clarify a response that the candidate has given to help you gain a better understanding of what he or she meant. This will require you to use probing questions that are not behavior-based; these are sometimes called open- or closed-ended questions. We discussed these earlier in the first slice. If it becomes necessary for you to probe, keep it focused on the "Can," the "Will," and the "Fit" for the job and stay off the rabbit trail!

Stay Off the Rabbit Trail

When I was a boy growing up in the South, expressing your thoughts in a wandering and disjointed way was called "going down a rabbit trail." I understood this idiom because, as a Southerner, I learned about actual rabbit trails.

In the woods, rabbits do not use any well-treaded paths. They blaze their own trails—and lots of them. These trails go all over the woods but collectively lead nowhere. If you ever tried to track a rabbit by following its trail through the woods (and I have), you will soon find yourself exhausted and confused.

When you ask probing questions, be careful that you don't "go down a rabbit trail." A "rabbit trail" probe can cause you to waste time, preventing you from asking some of the important questions you prepared in advance. Other times, "rabbit trails" can cause you to veer off the legal turf into a discussion about a protected class characteristic (race, color, religion, sex, national origin, age, or disability).

So if you must ask probing questions, make sure they are related to the job and are meant to find out about the candidate's skills, knowledge, work behaviors, and motivation to do the job (the "Can," the "Will," and the "Fit").

Another possibility is that the candidate goes down a rabbit trail. If this happens, redirect him or her. You may inform him or her that your question was not answered, ask if the question was understood, or ask whether you should repeat it.

A job-related example of a probing dialogue is presented below. In this example, the interviewer wants to find out how Sidney reacts to changing priorities. Sidney does not answer the question initially, so the interviewer probes for a more definitive response.

Interviewer: "Sidney, what do you do when priorities change quickly? Give an example of when this occurred. What was the result?" (*A behavior-based question.*)

Sidney: "I manage priorities every day in my job. That is what makes me so adept at managing my time."

Interviewer: "Have you ever had a situation when the priorities changed?" (*A closed-ended follow-up question.*)

Sidney: "Yes."

Interviewer: "Describe the most recent situation in which your priorities changed. How did you manage the change? What was the outcome?" (*Re-stating the original behavior-based question.*)

Sidney: "I delayed working on the next year's projections because my boss told me sales were down and we might be facing budget cuts. I used the time to develop a spreadsheet of areas we could cut in case we were asked to make reductions."

Interviewer: "How was the spreadsheet used? What was your boss's response?" (*Probing question.*)

Sidney: "Well, within a week after I completed the spreadsheet, we were actually asked to make reductions. The spreadsheet was used to prioritize which areas to cut. My boss thanked me for being so proactive."

Keep It Appropriate

As mentioned earlier, you should always ask questions that are appropriate and steer clear of inappropriate discussions, even if the candidate raises an inappropriate topic. If the candidate brings up an issue that is unadvisable (such as comments about children or church involvement) during the interview, you should respond politely and shift the conversation back to a work and job-related discussion.

For example, you could say: "Thank you for volunteering that information, but let's focus on your qualification for the job." Make a written note that the candidate raised the particular issue and that you turned the interview back to a business-oriented conversation. Remember, inappropriate questions or discussions are those that include a protected class characteristic (such as race, color, religion, sex, national origin, age or disability).

I discussed EEOC guidelines on proper interview questions and several protected class characteristics in PREPARE, the first slice of the book. The guidelines presented in that slice illustrated why certain questions are inappropriate under the law. The quick reference guide on the following page includes additional appropriate and inappropriate questions that were not discussed in the first slice. You may find it to be a useful reference to have on hand during the actual interview.

Quick Reference Guide

	APPROPRIATE	**INAPPROPRIATE**
Education	What is your academic, vocational, or professional education attainment?	None
Experience	Describe your work experience.	None
Language	Do you speak, read, or write a foreign language? (*Note: This question is appropriate **only** if this ability is relevant to the performance of the job.*)	What is your native language? What do you speak at home? How did you learn to speak, read, or write a foreign language?
Military Exp.	Have you served in the U.S. Military? Describe your experience.	Have you served in the Military of a country other than the U.S.?
Name	Have you ever worked for this company under a different name? Is there additional information concerning change of name, use of an assumed name, or nickname necessary to check your work record?	Have you ever worked under another name, and if so, where and when? What is your maiden name? Have you ever changed your name?
Organization	What organizations or memberships do you use to remain current and informed in your field of expertise?	Do you belong to any clubs or social organizations? Do you hold membership in any religious, community, or social groups? What society, clubs, or lodges do you belong to?
References	Who referred you to the company? Can you provide names of people who are willing to provide professional and (or) character references for you?	Can you provide the name of your pastor, priest, rabbi, or other religious associates as a reference? (*Note: This question **may** be appropriate for a candidate applying for a job with a religious organization.*)
Relatives	Do you have any relatives currently employed by the organization?	What are the names, addresses, ages, and telephone numbers of relatives not employed by the organization?

Confirm Evidence

As the candidate responds to the interview questions, the interviewer will collect evidence of his or her qualifications to perform the job. This evidence will paint a positive or negative image of the candidate's future performance. The interviewer should seek to confirm that image.

For example, if you are getting a negative impression about the candidate's customer service skills, you might ask: "Tell me about a time when you were only required to provide a minimum level of customer service but you went over and beyond what you were required to do." By asking this question, you are seeking evidence to confirm or negate your initial impression and will get a clearer picture of how he or she will actually perform.

Manage the Interview

Interviewing, like many other processes, requires you to orchestrate several tasks at the same time, which will test your management skills. As I mentioned earlier, sometimes a candidate will stray from the topic, ramble, or go down a rabbit trail during the interview. If this occurs, use the following methods to get the candidate back on topic:

- ✓ Explain that time is limited and you want to make sure to cover all of the information
- ✓ Redirect the interview by tactfully asking the next question
- ✓ Follow up with a closed-ended question

Allow for Reflection

Behavior-based questions will require the candidate to think about the question and formulate a response. Do not rush the candidate to respond quickly to your questions; wait for the answer and provide ample time for him or her to respond. If you interrupt the candidate or move to the next question when he or she falls silent, important information may not be revealed. Tell the candidate that it is OK to reflect.

For example, at the beginning of the interview, you could say: "I want to hear all the important parts of your answers, so don't feel that you have to rush your answers." If the candidate fails to answer after an ample time period, say, about 20 seconds, you should ask if clarification is needed, or if he or she needs you to repeat the question. For behavior-based questions—which are harder to answer well—reflection will help candidates give the best answers they can, thus helping you select the best-fit candidate.

Look for Stress Indicators

While conducting the interview, look for nonverbal cues from the candidate. A candidate who displays any of the nonverbal cues below could suggest that he or she may not be able to handle a stressful or demanding job. It could also indicate that the candidate is not providing truthful responses to your questions (or that he or she is nervous).

- ✓ Shifting of body
- ✓ Hesitations or stuttering
- ✓ Nervous laughter
- ✓ Excessive requests to rephrase questions
- ✓ Sweaty forehead or armpits
- ✓ Blotches of redness on the neck
- ✓ Shortness of breath
- ✓ Poor eye contact
- ✓ Shortness of responses

If you notice any of these behaviors during the interview, try to get to the bottom of it. You should try to put the candidate at ease, perhaps by offering him or her something to drink or allowing a brief pause in the questioning. You could also rephrase your questions and ask the candidate for feedback to ensure that he or she clearly understood your questions.

Close the Interview

The manner in which an interview is opened sets the tone; the way it is closed sets the impression. This impression will cast a positive or negative image of the hiring manager and the organization in the mind of the candidate. Taking the time to answer the candidate's questions, explain next steps, and preview the job contribute to leaving a positive impression on the candidate.

Answer Questions and Discuss Next Steps

As mentioned earlier, communication during the interview should not be one-way. Although two-way interaction takes place throughout the interview, candidates often have specific questions for the hiring manager. Make sure you reserve enough time at the end of the interview to answer questions.

Before closing the interview, thank the candidate for his or her time and express that you appreciate him or her choosing to interview with your organization.

Finally, make sure you inform the candidate of the next steps in the hiring process and when he or she should expect to hear from you or a representative from the organization. Escorting the candidate to the next interview, the elevator, or back to the reception area is also a nice touch. It shows professionalism and ensures that the candidate does not get lost finding his or her way from the interview. More importantly, it helps you to maintain your rapport with the candidate, which enhances the image of your organization.

Give a Realistic Job Preview

After each interview, provide the candidate with a realistic job preview. An example of a realistic job preview is allowing the candidate to visit or tour the work area of the company and/or talk with employees who are currently performing the job or have performed the job in the past. You may also show a video of the real work environment.

A realistic job preview presents candidates with both positive and negative information about the job, not just the good parts. This information allows candidates to choose for themselves, according to their needs, whether to continue the hiring process. Realistic information also reduces employee turnover by creating pre-employment expectations consistent with post-employment work requirements. This results in initial employee engagement, job satisfaction, and commitment to the organization.

So, you have mastered your interview sessions. You are exhausted from asking the same questions over and over again (and you can probably still hear the voices of all the candidates in your head). The result of those interviews is a stack of papers with plenty of notes that you have gathered from each candidate. At this point, you should be thinking about next step: evaluating and selecting the best-fit employee!

The Third Slice—EVALUATE

Take a deep breath. You've done great! You are now in the home stretch of the hiring process. As you complete the interview with each candidate, you move closer to the finish line. This part of the hiring process will require you to evaluate the candidates, first individually and then collectively, to compare their qualifications and select the best-fit. Then, after confirming favorable background and reference checks, you will be ready to make the job offer. The tasks below will help you navigate this phase:

- ☐ **Evaluate Each Candidate**
- ☐ **Rank the Candidates**
- ☐ **Select the Best Fit**
- ☐ **Check Background and References**
- ☐ **Screen for Drugs**
- ☐ **Extend the Job Offer**

EVALUATE EACH CANDIDATE

Evaluate the performance of the candidate immediately following the interview. You should not delay this part of the process; complete it while it is still fresh in your mind. Although this is meant to be an evaluation of each candidate individually, you should use a method that will standardize your evaluation for all candidates who interviewed for the job. You should allow yourself at least 15 minutes immediately after the interview to perform this task.

Many organizations use an evaluation form to both standardize and facilitate the evaluation process. This helps to create consistency in the evaluation and reduces the chance of legal action against the organization for unfair hiring practices. Examples of completed excerpts from the Hiring Workbook are shown on the following pages. (You can find the entire blank Hiring Workbook on the book's website.)

Excerpts from Page 1 of Hiring Workbook (Completed)

Candidate Name Sam Smith   **Position** Administrative Asst.

Required Skills & Knowledge (THE "CAN")	VERY STRONG	STRONG	AVG.	WEAK	VERY WEAK	
Communications (Written & Verbal)	☐	☒	☐	☐	☐	❶
Clerical Competency	☒	☐	☐	☐	☐	❷
Organization/Planning/Prioritization	☒	☐	☐	☐	☐	❸
Attention to Detail	☐	☒	☐	☐	☐	❹
Office Management	☒	☐	☐	☐	☐	❺

Comments

❶ Response to questions and examples of documents show strong written & verbal communication skills.

❷ Work examples indicate very strong clerical skills.

❸ A very solid organizer and planner. Evidence of excellent prioritization of work.

❹ Response to questions gave examples of strong attention to detail.

❺ Evidence of very strong skills in office management (current position).

Excerpts from Page 2 of Hiring Workbook (Completed)

Candidate Name Sam Smith   **Position** Administrative Asst.

Required Work Behaviors (THE "FIT")	VERY STRONG	STRONG	AVG.	WEAK	VERY WEAK	
Interpersonal Relationships	☒	☐	☐	☐	☐	❶
Learning Agility and Innovation	☒	☐	☐	☐	☐	❷
Dealing With Ambiguity	☐	☒	☐	☐	☐	❸
Managing Diversity	☐	☒	☐	☐	☐	❹
Stress Tolerance	☒	☐	☐	☐	☐	❺

Comments

❶ Clear evidence of strong interpersonal skills—a people person.

❷ Examples of quickly learning new concepts and innovative ways of doing things.

❸ Seems to have a knack for shifting gears quickly and acting under uncertainty.

❹ Provided examples of dealing equitably and effectively with all cultures, ages, and genders.

❺ Examples of very strong coping skills to deal with stress inside/outside of work.

Excerpts from Page 3 of Hiring Workbook (Completed)

Candidate Name   Sam Smith   **Position**   Administrative Asst.

Candidate's Motivation to Do the Job
(THE "WILL")

(For example, are the duties and responsibilities consistent with the candidate's career goals? What type of work does he or she enjoy? Did the candidate do any research to learn about the company?)

BS Degree in Office Management. Administrative Assistant to the President in current job. Sam seems to enjoy working with people and doing administrative work. This position is consistent with her career goal (worked in and learned from a variety of Administrative Assistant positions with increasing levels of responsibilities).

Candidate's Strengths and Weaknesses

Weaknesses include no experience in the Dairy Industry and not used to working in a matrix organization. However, given her skillset, she should be able to quickly overcome these weaknesses.

Strengths include clerical, organizing, planning, prioritizing and office management. A personable business professional with impeccable interpersonal skills. Sam has very strong learning agility, innovation skills, and stress tolerance. A very strong candidate overall.

OVERALL RATING	VERY STRONG	STRONG	AVG.	WEAK	VERY WEAK
	☒	☐	☐	☐	☐

DECISION	RECOMMEND	DO NOT RECOMMEND
	☒	☐

COMMENTS   Request background check and call to extend offer once approved.

When evaluating the candidate, you should evaluate him or her from the perspective of how questions were answered, not just the words the candidate used. If you interviewed the candidate as part of a panel, discuss his or her interview performance with the other panel members and include their feedback as part of the candidate's evaluation. Generally, you should consider:

- ✓ Depth of responses
- ✓ Proper expressiveness
- ✓ Pace and energy level
- ✓ Good eye contact
- ✓ Consistency of responses
- ✓ Ability to state both sides of an issue, then take a stand
- ✓ Openness and candor
- ✓ Level of interest in the job and company
- ✓ Past work behavior

Also, questions that the candidates ask are just as important as their responses to the questions you ask. Consider the quality of the questions and whether or not they express interest in the job and company. The depth of a candidate's questions also informs you of his or her knowledge of the company and of the job he or she is seeking. You must consider your total interview experience with the candidate in order to perform an individual evaluation of his or her qualifications for the job (the "Can"), motivation to perform the job (the "Will"), and fit for the culture (the "Fit").

Qualifications for the Job (the "Can")

Review all the information you have gathered from the **Prepare** and **Interview** phases about the candidate's competency level and ability to perform the job. The candidate's résumé and answers to your interview questions will highlight his or her education, job related experience, and skills required to perform the job. The background check that you will perform later should corroborate this information.

Motivation to Perform the Job (the "Will")

Review evidence from the interview to determine if the candidate is motivated to be a part of the organization and to perform the requirements of the job. For example, did the candidate present evidence during the interview that he or she conducted any research about the organization? Did you determine that the job was consistent with and supported the career goals of the candidate?

Fit for the Culture (the "Fit")

Again, assessing fit is of paramount importance when evaluating candidates for a job. When evaluating the candidate, consider his or her work behavior (for example, preference to work autonomously or in teams) and style and whether they are a fit for the culture.

This does not mean that you should always select the candidate who has the same work style as everyone else in the organization. Sometimes the best-fit candidate is the one who brings a unique perspective to the workplace (for example, a different personality). So, assess the strengths, weaknesses, and overall needs of the team to ensure that the potential employee will fit in well.

A great deal of emphasis should be placed on complementary strengths and experience that the candidate brings to the team. Make sure that these are existing strengths and that the candidate can use them immediately; do not rely on his or her "potential" strengths. This will be especially important if you will require a candidate to hit the ground running once he or she starts.

Considering fit will not only benefit the organization; it will motivate the employee to perform at a high level. Motivation positively influences work attitude, commitment to the organization, and job satisfaction.

Based on Abraham Maslow's Hierarchy of Needs theory, people are motivated to satisfy certain lower-level needs first (things like food, water, shelter, and safety). Then once those needs are satisfied, they will seek to satisfy mid-level needs (such as belonging and self-esteem). After those needs are met, they will pursue the need to become self-actualized. Self-actualization is the highest level of need to be satisfied. Person-organization fit seems to result in employees meeting both lower- and higher-level needs, which can lead to well-being and the achievement of self-actualization.

Assessments as an Evaluation Tool

Assessments are becoming increasingly popular as a tool to evaluate and select the best-fit candidate. These instruments are varied and are used to measure candidates' skills and knowledge (the "Can"), motivation and values (the "Will"), work behavior, personality and emotional intelligence (the "Fit"), and other factors. Assessments are usually administered by someone specifically certified to use them. If your company uses assessments to evaluate candidates, and you are not certified to administer any instrument necessary to assess the candidates you are interviewing, you should contact HR to determine who is certified to administer that particular instrument.

If you will use assessments as part of the evaluation process, keep in mind that they must be relevant to the job for which the candidates are applying. And, if you are evaluating several candidates for the same job, the same assessments must be administered to all the candidates you evaluate for that job. This practice will avoid unfair treatment of any protected classes.

Some companies use assessments to screen out candidates. In other words, a candidate cannot progress in the hiring process if he or she does not pass or produce an acceptable result. As the hiring manager, however, you should be mindful that assessment results don't always give a clear picture of the candidate. One reason for this is that the candidate may be experiencing stress or other types of mental or environmental issues outside of his or her control that may affect the results of the assessment.

In my opinion, assessment results should only be one measure of potential success of a candidate. The candidate's proven work experience, motivation, and work behavior should be weighed heavily. If hiring managers only use the results of an assessment to make a final evaluation of a candidate, they could miss out on selecting the best-fit candidate.

RANK THE CANDIDATES

At some point during the evaluation phase, you will have to compare and contrast your evaluations of the candidates with each other. Some interviewers wait until all the candidates have been interviewed to evaluate them collectively.

One way to accomplish this is to create a table with the required skills, knowledge, and work behaviors as the column headings. Assign each candidate a row of the table. Then, populate each row with the information you have gathered after all the candidates have interviewed. Once completed, the table can then be used to compare the candidates to each other. It will also allow you to rank the candidates according to their interview performance, skills and knowledge, and work behaviors.

While this method of ranking the candidates is effective, it requires more effort than a rank-as-you-go method. Using the rank-as-you-go method to evaluate candidates will allow you to compare the candidates with one another as you progress through the interviews. Using the rank-as-you-go system, once the last interview has been completed, you will have already completed the ranking of all the candidates who interviewed for the job. This is both an effective and efficient approach for collectively evaluating the candidates. (After all, I did promise to make hiring easy as PIE!)

The Candidate Ranking Matrix, shown below, is a rank-as-you-go form that I have used to indicate rankings for multiple candidates. (Use it in conjunction with the Hiring Workbook.) Immediately after each interview, review the comments, overall rating, and decision to hire rating that the candidate received in the Hiring Workbook. Ask yourself the following questions:

- ✓ What are this candidate's strengths?
- ✓ What are his or her weaknesses?
- ✓ Will this candidate have to acquire additional skills to perform the job, or is he or she able to perform the job now?
- ✓ How does this candidate compare to the other candidates who were interviewed?

Answers to these questions should provide the information necessary to rank each candidate. Then, on the Candidate Ranking Matrix, place the candidate in rank order, according to his or her qualifications. An example of the Candidate Ranking Matrix is shown below.

Example

Use the matrix below to rank candidates when conducting multiple interviews. After **each** interview, rank **all** candidates you've seen according to his or her interview performance, qualifications, and fit for the job/culture.

	1	2	3	4
First Candidate	Jordan Miller			
Second Candidate's Rank Order	Jordan Miller	Pat Jones		
Third Candidate's Rank Order	Sam Smith	Jordan Miller	Pat Jones	
Fourth Candidate's Rank Order	Sam Smith	Jordan Miller	Avery Martinez	Pat Jones

SELECT THE BEST FIT

In the Ranking Matrix you just reviewed, Sam Smith was the best-fit candidate and, if everything goes well with the remaining portion of this phase of the hiring process, Sam will likely become the best-fit employee.

At this stage, you are now on the cusp of making your best-fit decision. Are you confident who the best-fit candidate is? Why do you really think this candidate is the best fit?

According to research in social psychology, similarity-attraction can bias the selection of the best-fit candidate. In other words, if the candidate's personality, age, gender, or attitudes are similar to your own, you may evaluate the candidate too positively relative to ability, motivation, and job fit. You have to be conscious of this phenomenon to be sure you're making objective evaluations.

To review, select the best-fit candidate for the job and company culture by following these procedures:

- ✓ Analyze the Candidate Ranking Matrix
- ✓ Review the Hiring Workbook for each candidate again, if necessary
- ✓ Make a final decision about the best-fit candidate

CHECK BACKGROUND AND REFERENCES

Once you have selected a finalist for the job, you should check the candidate's background to verify the accuracy of the information presented on his or her résumé and during the interview.

The candidate's written permission to do a background check is required before proceeding. HR usually obtains this authorization.

Although most of the required background check information can be purchased on the Internet, most HR departments outsource this part of the process to a professional pre-employment screening agency.

Sometimes HR will conduct all or part of the background check internally, depending on the company. If you don't have an HR department, you will need to determine how much of the background check you will do yourself, if any.

Whether you conduct the background check yourself or outsource it to a professional, it should be completed before formalizing the job offer. On occasions, however, the need to fill a critical position right away will necessitate you making the job offer before the results of the background check are in. This is an acceptable hiring practice, but in these cases, you should always make the job offer contingent upon the candidate receiving a favorable background check.

Hiring managers should be mindful, however, of the risks associated with contingent offers. If the candidate does not pass the background check after receiving a contingent offer, his or her employment is terminated as previously agreed. For this reason, contingent offers are best made by HR whenever possible—and not by someone new to hiring.

Criminal History

In addition to providing information about work history and education, the background check will also reveal whether or not the candidate has any criminal convictions. These convictions fall into two categories: felonies and misdemeanors.

A candidate with a felony conviction is usually not viewed favorably for hiring, depending on the job requirement and company policy. For example, if a candidate for a bank teller job has a conviction for, say, theft of large sums of money (a felony), he or she will not likely be hired by a bank. That same candidate, on the other hand, might be considered for certain positions in a construction company or a restaurant.

Misdemeanors are usually not judged with as much severity as felonies. Many companies don't take the time to check for misdemeanors, although they legally can. If you are going to use a candidate's criminal conviction as the basis for not extending an offer, you should consult with legal counsel first, as many state laws restrict the situations in which companies can refuse to hire someone because of a criminal conviction, even a felony.

Reference Checks

Although reference checks can be outsourced along with the other pre-employment checks, many of them are conducted internally by HR or the hiring manager. The references' contact information is usually provided by the candidate during the application process. These references may include former bosses, co-workers, and others with knowledge of the candidate's job performance.

Many of us have received phone calls from members of hiring organizations asking us about our knowledge of a candidate they were vetting for a job. The person calling will typically ask to verify the candidate's job title, tenure, and his or her performance in that role. The caller may even ask if you, the person listed as a reference, would hire or be willing to work with that person again.

While some reference checkers go beyond these simple questions, answers to the above questions usually provide all the information you need to make a final hiring decision. Three to six reference checks should be sufficient to gather enough information to identify the performance pattern of the candidates.

Screen for Drugs

Most employers require pre-employment drug screening for candidates identified as finalists. Because of the expertise required to perform drug screening, most companies outsource it.

There are different types of drug tests that candidates may be asked to take as part of the drug screening process. These may include urine, blood, hair, and saliva tests, with the most common one being the urinalysis test, which detects illegal substances. Identifying those who use illegal substances early in the hiring process allows organizations to work towards a drug-free workplace.

This not only protects the business but improves employee morale and productivity, while decreasing accidents, downtime, and turnover. As with background and reference checks, you may have to fill a critical position before receiving the results of the drug screening. Again, this is acceptable, but make sure the job offer is contingent upon the candidate receiving a clean drug test.

Extend the Offer

Extending the job offer is the final step, and for me, the most exciting part of the hiring process. And if you have made a positive impression on the candidate, this will be an exciting time for him or her too. Like crossing the finish line at the end of a foot race, it can be an exhilarating conclusion for the hiring manager—and the candidate.

When extending an offer, phone the selected candidate and present the offer verbally. This goes a long way to close the deal. Then, send the selected candidate an offer letter, containing all offer specifics, as well as a job description.

Phone the Final Candidate

Identify a time to phone the selected candidate that is convenient for both of you. The offer process should not be rushed, so make sure you set aside enough time for this important part of the hiring process.

Do not call the selected candidate "cold turkey" to extend the offer; prepare first. You have gleaned loads of information about the selected candidate during the hiring process; review this information again. This time, look for information that will make your offer more persuasive (for example, the company's ability to meet career goals, salary expectation, and available start date and willingness to reimburse relocation costs).

Do you remember waiting to be called for your dream job? Do you remember actually getting the call? Do you remember listening intently for and hearing that you were selected for the job?

Phone the selected candidate and present the offer with enthusiasm. Let him or her know that you feel he or she will be a great addition to the team and will have a promising future with your organization. This will set the tone for the rest of the discussion and the relationship with your soon-to-be-employee. Remember, this is still a two-way discussion with interested parties; the selected candidate has not yet accepted the offer at this point. Be sure to explain the offer details thoroughly and allow the selected candidate to ask questions along the way.

Provide Offer Details

Give the selected candidate the following information:

- ✓ The 'official offer' and the exact job title
- ✓ Compensation (starting salary and bonus target, if applicable)

✓ Reporting relationships (that is, to whom he or she will report and whether or not he or she will have direct reports)
✓ Coverage of relocation cost, if any
✓ Explain that the offer is contingent on successfully passing the background check and/or drug screening, if not already completed

Explain Benefits

The compensation package may also include benefits. Some hiring managers are not comfortable explaining this part of the offer and therefore rely upon HR to explain it.

But not you! Since you identified the compensation details when you investigated the job specifications, you are armed and ready to present this information to the candidate. And good for you—explaining the benefits yourself presents a professional image of you and the company to the candidate. When explaining the benefits to the candidate, use the checklist below as a guideline to ensure you cover the required items:

Additional Compensation
✓ 401k and percentage of match, if applicable
✓ Profit sharing
✓ Pension, if applicable
✓ Other

Benefits & Effective Start Date
✓ Medical
✓ Dental
✓ Vision
✓ Flexible Spending Account
✓ Other

Time Off
- ✓ Vacation
- ✓ Personal
- ✓ Sick
- ✓ Paid Time Off (PTO), if applicable
- ✓ Other

Offer a Reasonable Answer Period

The selected candidate may not be prepared to accept the job offer immediately after receiving it on the phone. This may mean that the candidate is considering other offers or is having second thoughts about leaving his or her current employment or might not be sure about working for your company. He or she may just require more time to talk with family members about the new opportunity and to think it over before making a decision. He or she may just want to make an informed decision, as you did. Whatever the reason, you should offer a reasonable job offer decision period, which is usually determined by the company's policy.

The level of urgency to fill the position should also be considered. However, if you apply too much pressure to the candidate, you may receive a rejection, particularly if you did not disclose the urgency to fill the position during your "next steps" discussion at the close of the interview. Each time you speak with a candidate, you should ensure that you both understand the next steps and timing.

Send an Offer Letter

As mentioned earlier, send an official offer letter to the final candidate. Company policy will guide when the offer letter is sent. Some organizations send the offer letter immediately, once the decision to hire the finalist is made. Some send the offer letter after the verbal offer is made by phone and an acceptance is uncertain. Others wait to send the official offer letter along with other documents (such as benefits information, work schedule, and job description) once the candidate verbally agrees to accept the job offer.

Regardless of when the offer letter is sent, it should contain the same information presented in the verbal offer. The offer letter should be signed by you or another authorized person from your company. Once the final candidate accepts the job offer, ask him or her to sign and return the offer letter.

You should be mindful that negotiations often ensue after the initial offer, depending on the level of the job. These negotiations may be related to salary, start dates, benefits, bonus targets, relocation package, etc. You may have one or two discussions with the candidate to reach a place where you mutually feel comfortable. If you cannot reach an agreement, you may have to rescind the offer and move to the next qualified candidate.

Welcome the New Employee Aboard

Once the candidate accepts the job offer, welcome him or her aboard your organization. Let your new employee know that you are excited about his or her decision to accept the job offer. Reiterate that he or she will be a great addition to the team. Explain the on-boarding process and what performance support is available. You should also review specific details about the final candidate's new department and what role he or she is expected to play.

For other candidates you have interviewed, ensure that you or someone from HR follow-up with them to thank them and let them know they were not selected. If you want a good generic explanation, it could be: "We had a number of qualified applicants and we selected the candidate that most closely matched our needs." Wish them well in the job search—after all, they made it to the final stages and you may want to consider them for other roles in the future.

Since the finalists have invested more time interviewing with your company, it is a nice touch for the hiring manager to reach out to them personally to thank them for their time. Sometimes, when you do that, candidates may ask where they went wrong during the interview. Be careful not to get involved in rehashing the interview and going down any dangerous rabbit trails. Let the candidate know that everyone who interviewed was fairly assessed against the needs of the company. While his or her skills and experiences were impressive, you chose someone who best met the needs of the company.

Conclusion

Hiring Made Easy as PIE presents a turnkey approach for hiring. Following this process ensures structure and consistency that will help you stay the course for hiring the best-fit employee, regardless of the internal or external influences to hire a particular candidate. As a hiring manager, I have felt the influence to hire a particular candidate, even when the influence was unspoken.

I was once asked to serve as a member of an interview panel to select an HR Manager. My task was to help interview the two candidates who were finalists for the job. One of the candidates, whom I will refer to as Christina, was also endorsed by one of our senior managers (Christina had worked with that senior manager at another company). I must admit that my colleague's endorsement of her impressed me and influenced my perception of her before we met. Accordingly, I expected her to be well-qualified and prepared for the interview.

While reviewing Christina's résumé, I noticed that she completed the same master's degree program as I did . . . and from the same university! I felt really good about Christina.

At the beginning of the interview with her, I mentioned this coincidence to help build rapport. She excitedly exclaimed that she loved that program and had enjoyed all the courses. I asked her what her favorite course had been. Her response was, "I don't remember the name of the course, but it was one of Professor Davis's classes."

Her response gave me pause; my initial impression of her comment was that something about her qualifications had been misleading. I sought to confirm evidence for another item on her résumé and discovered yet another misleading claim. Christina had indicated that she was a member of a prominent industry-specific organization. When I asked if she found the monthly meetings helpful for her job, she said, "I'm not an active member. I just joined as a student because the professor asked me to do so." She had not written "inactive member" on her résumé, however.

Although she otherwise appeared qualified for the job and was endorsed by one of our senior managers, the inconsistencies I found led me to believe that she might have a tendency to embellish the truth. I concluded that she was not a fit for the job or our culture. The funny thing is that the other two interviewers independently came to the same conclusion.

Then it came time for the interview with the second candidate. The second candidate—let's call her Jamie—showed up 10 minutes late. She was sweating and appeared somewhat disheveled from rushing. As soon as I introduced myself to her, she apologized and began explaining why she was late for the interview. She explained that she had started out on time but inadvertently locked herself out of her house, with her car key still inside the house. After circling the house several times looking for a way in, she found a window unlocked and crawled through it to retrieve the key for her car.

Jamie responded to the interview questions with lots of details, so we were able to confirm the information on her résumé. Not only did she possess the skills, knowledge, and experience necessary for the job, but she also exhibited the "it factor" (work behaviors) necessary to be successful in the job.

The interview panel unanimously agreed to extend the job offer to Jamie. As of this writing, 16 years later, she is still with the same company.

Earlier, we discussed internal influences that may cloud our judgment, such as the similarity-attraction phenomenon. This story presents an example of an external influence—in this case, another person's influence—that may also cloud our judgment about selecting the best-fit candidate.

The good news is you now have a structured process to help you steer clear of those influences, both internal and external. If I had not used a structured interview, the influence that I initially felt as a result of the senior manager's endorsement of Christina might have won out—but, fortunately, it did not.

Perfecting and following the structured hiring process, as presented in *Hiring Made Easy as PIE*, guided me through the interview example above. It alleviated the influence I felt to hire a specific candidate and stay on the "legal turf," while selecting the best-fit employee. Through many years of experience and research, I have synthesized complex hiring practices into an easy-to-follow process. I wrote this book as a hiring guide to share this process with others.

My hope is that the hiring process presented in this book will serve others as well it has served me and that it will make Hiring **Easy as PIE.**

Resources

Blank Hiring Workbook (available for download on website)
Candidate Ranking Matrix (available for download on website)
Sample Behavior-Based Questions (on the following pages)

To download free copies of these resources, or to purchase this book, visit our website at:

www.HiringMadeEasyasPie.com

Sample Behavior-Based Questions

Remember, the goal of an interview is to determine three things about the candidate:

1. Can the candidate do the job?

Does the candidate have required skills, knowledge, education and experience for this position? Has he or she been able to articulate real experience-based scenarios to demonstrate the skills, knowledge and other requirements for the job?

The following are examples of questions that can be used to determine if the candidate can do the job:

- ✓ "Describe the most important skills that have led to your success in the position for which you are applying. Recount how you have used those skills during your career. What has been their impact on your career?"

- ✓ "Tell me about a time when a supervisor gave you feedback concerning a skills weakness. What actions did you take and what was the outcome?"

- ✓ "Explain how you could leverage your knowledge, skills, and experience to improve performance in the position for which you are applying. How would you implement your plan of action? What do you think will be the result the first year?"

- ✓ "Tell me about a time when you did not have the resources you needed to perform the job successfully. What resources were you lacking? What actions did you take to solve the resource problem? What were the results?"

✓ "Describe the knowledge and skills that team members would need to possess to be successful. What have you done to ensure that your team members possess the necessary skills to be successful? What was the result?"

✓ "Tell me about a time when you did not have the knowledge and skills to excel in the job. What did you do? What was the result?"

✓ "Describe your experience performing xyz task? What approach would you take to perform the critical tasks for the position you are applying? What result would you expect initially and over time?"

✓ "Tell me about a time when there was a need to improve the way a certain aspect of your job was performed. What was that aspect of your job that required improvement? What did you do and what was the result?"

✓ "Tell me about a time when you had to help your team members accomplish a task. What was the task? What was your contribution? How did it turn out?"

✓ "How do the knowledge, skills and experience that you will bring to the job contribute to the overall success of the organization?"

2. Will the candidate do the job?

Is the candidate motivated? Are job requirements consistent with what the candidate enjoys doing? Do the person's career objectives align with the duties of the job, or are there advancement opportunities? Does the candidate job history evidence the type of upward advancement you would expect for someone holding his or her current position or the position for which the candidate is seeking?

The following are examples of questions that can be used to determine if the candidate will do the job:

✓ "What are your career goals? What are you doing to achieve them? In what way will this job contribute to achieving them?"

✓ "Give me an example of a situation that required you to do more than what was required of you on the job. What actions did you take? What difference did your actions make?"

✓ "There are times when we work without close supervision or support to get the job done. Tell me about a time when you found yourself in such a situation. How did things turn out?"

✓ "Which aspects of the job we are discussing energize you? On the flip side, tell me which part would not be your favorite."

✓ "From your experience, what do you expect will be the greatest challenge you will face that will impact your success in this position? What will you do to overcome these challenges? How do you think the strategies will turn out?"

✓ "Tell me about a time when you had to motivate team members to accomplish a task. How did you motivate them? How did you feel about motivating your team members?"

✓ "Explain what you have done in the past to hone your skills in the position for which you are applying. How have those actions benefitted you?"

✓ "Describe the importance of this job to the success of the organization."

✓ "Explain your plans to continually improve in this position? How will you implement your plans? What do you think will be the result?"

✓ "If you were not working in this field, what else would you be doing? Explain why?"

✓ "If offered this position, what changes would you like to make, if any? How do you see those changes impacting the job five years from now?"

3. Is the candidate a Fit for the culture?

Is the candidate a good fit for the job as well as the culture within the organization? Specifically, does his or her work behavior, style, and personality mesh with the job and the culture?

The following are examples of questions that can be used to determine if the candidate is a good fit for the job and culture:

✓ "Describe an important project you worked on with team members who had different work styles from you. How did you overcome the differences and what was the outcome?"

✓ "Recall for me a work situation in which you felt that your values might be compromised. How did you work through the situation and what was the outcome?"

✓ "Tell me about a time when you were under stress on the job. How did you work through it and what resulted from your actions?"

✓ "Describe the ideal work environment. How have you adapted in the past to a less than ideal work environment?"

✓ "Do you prefer to work on a team or as an individual contributor? Tell me about a time when you had to function in a less preferred role. What was the situation? How did it turn out?"

✓ "Describe the ideal supervisor that you have worked for in the past. What made that supervisor ideal? How did you relate to that supervisor?"

✓ "Tell me about a time when you had to make a decision without having all the information that was required. What was the situation? What was the impact of that decision?"

✓ "Tell me about a time when you had competing priorities. How did you handle the priorities? What was the result?"

✓ "Tell me about a time when team members were in conflict about how to accomplish a task. What actions did you take as a member of the team? How did the task get accomplished?"

✓ "Tell me about a time when your team did not successfully accomplish a given task. What was your role on the team? What were the results?"

Suggested Readings

Robert G. Burgess, *In the Field: An Introduction to Field Research* (London: Allen & Unwin, 1984).

Donn Byrne, "Interpersonal attraction and attitude similarity," *Journal of Abnormal and Social Psychology* 62 (1961), 713-715.

Donn Byrne, *The Attraction Paradigm* (New York: Academic Press, 1971).

Daniel M. Cable and Timothy A. Judge, "Person-organization fit, job choice decisions, and organizational entry," *Organizational Behavior and Human Decision Processes* 67, 294-311.

Kim S. Cameron and Robert E. Quinn, *Diagnosing and Changing Organizational Culture: Based on the Competing Values Framework* (Jossey-Bass, 2011). 3rd edition.

D'Vera Cohn and Paul Taylor, "Baby Boomers Approach 65 – Glumly: Survey Findings about America's Largest Generation" (Pew Research Center, 2010), http://www.pewsocialtrends. org/2010/12/20/baby-boomers-approach-65-glumly/

Laura Davis, "You Can't Ask That! Unmasking the Myths About 'Illegal' Pre-Employment Interview Questions," *ALSB Journal of Employment and Labor Law* 12 (2011), 39-57.

EEOC, "Pre-Employment Inquiries," accessed early 2015, http://www. eeoc.gov/laws/practices/index.cfm#pre-employment_inquiries

Robert D. Gatewood, Mary A. Gowan, and Gary J. Lautenschlager, "Corporate image, recruitment image, and initial job choice decisions," *Academy of Management Journal* 36 (1993), 414-427.

Laura M. Graves and Gary N. Powell, "The effect of sex similarity on recruiters' evaluations of actual applicants: A test of the similarity-attraction paradigm," *Personnel Psychology* 48 (1995), 85-98.

Herbert G. Heneman III. and Timothy A. Judge, *Staffing Organizations* (New York, NY: McGraw-Hill/Irwin, 2006). 5th edition.

Alonzo Johnson, Paul A. Winter, Thomas G. Reio, Henry L. Thompson, and Joseph M. Petrosko, "Managerial Recruitment: The Influence of Personality and Ideal Candidate Characteristics," *Journal of Management Development* 27 (2008), 631-648.

Amy L. Kristof, "Person-organization fit: An integrative review of its conceptualizations, measurement, and implications," *Personnel Psychology* 49 (2005), 1-49.

Abraham H. Maslow, "A theory of human motivation," *Psychological Review* 50 (1943), 370-396.

O'Net Online (2015). Summary Report for: 43-6014.00 - Secretaries and Administrative Assistants, Except Legal, Medical, and Executive. Retrieved from http://www.onetonline.org/link/summary/43-6014.00

Jeffrey S. Passel and D'Vera Cohn. "U.S. Population Projections: 2005–2050" (Pew Research Center, 2008), http://www.pewsocialtrends.org/2008/02/11/us-population-projections-2005-2050/

Society for Industrial and Organizational Psychology, "Principles for the Validation and Use of Personnel Selection Procedures"

(2003), retrieved from http://www.siop.org/_Principles/principlesdefault.aspx

Mary K. Suszko and James A. Breaugh, "The effects of realistic job previews on applicant self-selection and employee turnover, satisfaction, and coping ability," *Journal of Management* 12 (1986), 513-523.

Md. Mamin Ullah, "A Systematic Approach of Conducting Employee Selection Interview," *International Journal of Business and Management* 5 (2010), 106-112.

U.S. Department of Labor, Wage and Hour Division, Fact Sheet #17A: Exemption for Executive, Administrative, Professional, Computer & Outside Sales Employees Under the Fair Labor Standards Act (FLSA) (2008). Retrieved from http://www.dol.gov/whd/regs/compliance/fairpay/fs17a-overview.htm.

John P. Wanous, "Effects of a realistic job preview on job acceptance, job attitudes, and job survival," *Journal of Applied Psychology* 58 (1973), 327-332.

James D. Werbel and Jacqueline Landau, "The effectiveness of different recruitment sources: A mediating variable analysis," *Journal of Applied Psychology* 26 (1996), 1337-1350.

Charles R. Williams, Chalmer E. Labig and Thomas H. Stone, "Recruitment sources and posthire outcomes for job applicants and new hires: A test of two hypotheses," *Journal of Applied Psychology* 78 (1993), 163-172.

About the Author

Alonzo Johnson, Ph.D., is the Managing Partner of The OASYS Group, a talent management consulting company. He has held leadership positions in the military, higher education, and in the private business sector. Alonzo has over three decades of experience in talent management and human resources. His expertise includes staffing and organizational development.

Alonzo's vast experience in both researching and using hiring practices in business is scattered throughout this book. His research, which investigated methods of attracting employees with specific work behaviors to apply for a job, is published in the Journal of Management Development. He has developed training programs on employee selection for Fortune 500 companies and has taught leaders at all levels how to hire best-fit employees.

About The OASYS Group

The OASYS Group is a management consulting company. The mission of the company is to help people grow by providing talent management solutions for every stage of employment—from recruiting and onboarding new employees to engaging, developing, and retaining existing employees. The OASYS Group's core strategy is to align talent management processes with business goals. The competency-based approach creates a synchronized work environment in which employees are engaged, thereby increasing performance and reducing employee turnover.

The OASYS Group specializes in developing customized hiring processes for clients, and then training hiring managers to use those processes to select best-fit employees. The Company emphasizes the implications of conducting inappropriate interviews or asking unlawful questions. Accordingly, the focus is on formulating and asking appropriate questions during the interview phase. Hiring managers are also provided with customized checklists and job aids to use throughout the preparation, interviewing, and evaluation phases of the hiring process.

The OASYS Group offers an array of assessments to provide additional insights about the work behaviors of the potential employee.

Visit the company's website at www.TheOASYSGroup.com.